2010—2011中国保险市场年报

ANNUAL REPORT OF CHINA INSURANCE MARKET 2010–2011

目录

Contents

壹

主席致辞

2010 年，在党中央、国务院的正确领导下，中国保监会深入贯彻落实科学发展观，围绕“转方式、调结构、防风险、促发展”，开拓创新、扎实工作，在复杂多变的外部环境中抢抓机遇，有效巩固和扩大了应对国际金融危机冲击的成果，加快转变发展方式，着力推进科学监管、依法监管和有效监管，积极防范和化解风险，着力服务和保障民生，充分发挥保险的功能和作用，保险市场保持了良好的发展势头。

保险市场规模不断扩大

2010 年，全行业实现保费 14528 亿元[①]，同比增长 30.4%。财产险业务继续保持较快增长，实现保费 3895.6 亿元，同比增长 35.5%；人身险业务保费突破 1 万亿元，达到 10632.3 亿元，同比增长 28.7%。全年赔付金额 3200.4 亿元。保险业整体实力显著增强，截至 2010 年底，保险公司总资产突破 5 万亿元，达 50467.2 亿元；净资产 5208.9 亿元，比 2009 年底增加 604.1 亿元。保险资金运用余额达 4.6 万亿元，实现投资收益 2014.6 亿元，平均收益率为 4.84%。经营效益继续提升，保险公司利润总额达到 910.3 亿元，较上年增加 65.3 亿元。再保险业务承保质量明显改善。

加快转变行业发展方式

2010 年，保险业加快转变发展方式，不断提高行业科学发展能力。在指导思想和经营目标上，更加注重全面协调可持续发展；在发展战略和盈利模式上，更加注重承保和投资相匹配、业务拓展

① 除特殊说明外，本年报中财务数据均为执行《企业会计准则解释第 2 号》后的审计数据，保费及赔付金额均为业务口径统计数据。

和内部管理相适应；在考核指标和费用政策上，更加注重质量效益导向，更加注重理性经营、集约管理。继续推进结构调整，努力提升发展质量。通过完善评价指标体系、发挥偿付能力约束作用等方式，促进风险保障型和内含价值高的业务发展。非寿险投资型业务继续平稳回落，家财险、工程险等业务较快发展，同比分别增长 27.5%、37.4%。健康、养老等保障性强的传统业务日益受到重视，银行保险业务继续向期交业务转型，寿险新单期交保费同比增长 32.2%。全行业加大产品服务创新力度，开发新产品 9800 多个。在继续发挥传统销售渠道优势的基础上，电话销售得到快速发展，网络销售等符合年轻群体消费习惯的新兴销售模式也得到探索和拓展，形成了不同渠道相互补充、共同发展的良好局面。目前，行业转变发展方式的成效逐步显现，车险业务扭亏为盈，寿险业务内含价值不断提升。

有效防范和化解风险

2010 年，保险业积极采取措施防范和化解风险，维护保险市场安全稳健运行。部分保险公司通过多种形式充实资本金，改善了偿付能力状况，全年共有 46 家公司增资 331.7 亿元，8 家公司发行次级债 225.5 亿元。截至 2010 年底，偿付能力不达标的保险公司 6 家，比年初减少 2 家；不达标公司的偿付能力关键指标有明显改善。制定实施保险资金运用管理暂行办法及相关制度，保险资金运用行为得到规范，维护了保险资金运用的安全稳健。发布《保险公司内部控制基本准则》，推动保险公司加快建立健全内控管理组织体系，制定内控标准和流程，明确董事会、管理层、内控管理部门的职责和分工。完善动态偿付能力压力测试和现金流监测制度，改进风险识别和预警制度。推行保险公司全面风险管理，进一步健全防范风险的应急工作机制。推动保险公司建立案件问责制度，积极防范案件风险。发挥保险保障基金作用，对发生重大风险的公司实施风险处置和救济制度。通过派驻监管工作组、推动公司重组等方式，妥善处置了个别公司的风险。

加强和改进保险监管

2010 年，保险监管机构着力推进科学监管、依法监管和有效监管，促进保险业又好又快发展。完善监管制度，制定和修订 11 项部门规章和一系列规范性文件，对现行保险监管规章制度进行全面清理。从法人、高管、问责三方面入手，强化保险公司依法合规经营的自觉性和主动性。完善监管组织体系，加强信息化监管改进法人机构分类监管，建立分支机构分类监管制度，研究探索宏观审慎监管，与外资保险公司的母国监管机构加强交流沟通和监管合作。通过专项检查、重点检查、综合性检查等方式，进一步规范保险市场秩序。明确保险公司信息披露要求，建立健全保险服务标准和赔付程序公开制度，制定电话营销行为标准，指导行业建立车险信息共享机制和保单承保理赔信息自主查询制度，积极保护被保险人利益。

积极服务经济社会发展

2010 年，保险业紧紧围绕国家经济建设与社会发展事业，立足保障和服务民生，扩大保险覆盖面，提升保险业服务能力。农业保险覆盖的农户数达 1.4 亿户次，提供风险保障 3943.1 亿元，同比分别增长 5.2% 和 3.4%。承保品种和保障范围不断拓宽，服务地域扩展至所有省区市。农村小额保险覆盖范围扩大到 24 个省，目前参保人数已超过 2000 万人。出口信用保险提供风险保障金额超过 1 万亿元，同比增长 66.8%，支持的出口额占我国一般贸易出口总额的 22.8%。主动参与社会风险管理，实现责任保险保费 115.9 亿元，同比增长 25.7%。在青海玉树地震、黑龙江伊春空难、上海高层住宅火灾等重大灾害事故中，保险业积极履行赔付责任。在上海世博会、广州亚运会等重大活动中，保险业较好地发挥了风险保障功能，累计提供保险保障 3000 多亿元，保障人数近 500 万人次。积极参与社会保障体系建设，推动商业养老和健康保险专业化经营，加大产品创新力度，提高养老和健康保险服务水平。

2010 年，在国际金融危机的严重影响与国际、国内环境的深刻变化中，保险业取得了来之不易的成绩。借此机会，我代表保监会，向保险业全体干部职工和长期以来关心支持保险业发展的社会各界人士和海内外朋友表示衷心的感谢！

2011 年是“十二五”开局之年，保险业将全面贯彻党的十七届五中全会和中央经济工作会议精神，继续深入贯彻落实科学发展观，正确把握保险业面临的新形势，以科学发展为主题，以加快转变发展方式为主线，坚持依法监管、科学监管和有效监管，着力防范化解保险风险，着力规范保险市场秩序，着力保护被保险人利益，促进保险业平稳较快发展，为构建社会主义和谐社会和全面建设小康社会作出新的贡献！

中国保险监督管理委员会主席 吴定富

2011 年 5 月 20 日

贰

经济社会的进步和发展

- 经济社会发展取得新进步，保险市场发展空间日益拓宽
- 中国综合实力进一步增强，夯实了保险市场发展的基础
- 金融业持续平稳健康发展，促进经济发展能力快速提升

2010年，面对极为复杂的国内外经济环境和严峻自然灾害的挑战，中国实施应对国际金融危机一揽子计划，加快推进经济发展方式转变，巩固了经济社会发展的良好势头，为"十一五"画上了一个圆满的句号，为"十二五"开局奠定了坚实的基础。

经济社会的进步和发展

经济社会发展取得新进步，保险市场发展空间日益拓宽

2010年，我国战胜青海玉树强烈地震、甘肃舟曲特大山洪泥石流等重大自然灾害，成功举办上海世博会和广州亚运会，胜利完成"十一五"规划确定的主要目标和任务。社会主义政治建设、经济建设、文化建设、社会建设以及生态文明建设取得重大进展。

农业、农村发展基础巩固加强

围绕"稳粮保供给、增收惠民生、改革促统筹、强基增后劲"，进一步强化强农、惠农政策。中央财政用于"三农"支出8579.7亿元，比上年增长18.3%。坚持对种粮农民实行直接补贴，增加了农资综合补贴、良种补贴、农机具购置补贴。进一步提高重点粮食品种最低收购价，让农民得到更多实惠。大力发展农产品加工业，推动生产与市场对接。以农田水利为重点，加强农业基础设施建设。以良种培育为重点，加快农业科技创新和推广。发挥城市对农村的辐射带动作用，促进城镇化和新农村建设良性互动。启动新一轮农村电网改造，解决了6186万农村人口饮用水安全问题，农民生产生活设施建设加快。2010年，我国粮食实现连续第七年增产，农民收入持续较快增长，农村综合改革稳步推进，农村民生和农村经济取得新的进步，为保增长保民生保稳定提供了有力的基础支撑。

经济结构调整积极推进

2010年，我国经济运行总体平稳，质量效益明显改善。第一、第二、第三产业分别增长4.3%、12.2%和9.5%。进一步实施重点行业调整振兴规划，淘汰落后产能任务全面完成，工业结构调整取得积极进展。实施知识创新工程和技术创新工程，突破了一批产业发展急需的前沿技术、核心技术和关键装备技术，一大批科研成果实现了产业化，战略性新兴产业迅速成长，自主创新能力显著增强。基础设施和基础产业保障能力提升。区域发展的协调性增强。节能减排、生态建设和环境保护扎实推进。随着发展方式的加快转变和经济结构的升级调整，新的风险不断出现，对作为"经济助推器"和"社会稳定器"的保险业提出了更多新的要求。

民生建设成效显著

坚持经济发展与社会发展相协调，围绕改善民生谋发展。加大积极就业政策力度，积极稳妥推进医药卫生体制改革，加快实施国家助学制度，加强房地产市场调控，与民生相关的各项社会事业加快发展。2010年的就业状况是国际金融危机发生以来最好的一年，全年城镇新增就业人口1168万人，年底城镇登记失业率4.1%，全国农民工总量比上年增长5.4%。中央财政用在与人民群众生活直接相关的教育、医疗卫生、社会保障和就业、住房保障方面的支出分别达到2547.3亿元、1485.4亿元、3785亿元和1125.7亿元，分别比上年增长28.6%、16.7%、14.8%和15%。

社会保障体系日益完善

社会保障水平进一步提高，社会保障面继续扩大。2010年底，全国参加城镇基本养老保险人数达到25673万人，比上年底增加2123万人。参加城镇基本医疗保险的人数43206万人，增加3059万人。新型农村合作医疗覆盖面进一步扩大，参合率达96.3%，医疗基金支出总额为832亿元，累计受益7.0亿人次。全国列入国家新型农村社会养老保险试点地区参保人数10277万人。最低生活保障、最低工资、失业保险、基本养老金、优抚对象补助、家庭经济困难学生资助等多项社会救助和保障标准得到提高，社会保障由以往只重视量的增加向既重视量的增加又重视质的提高转变。

中国综合实力进一步增强，夯实了保险市场发展的基础

国民经济形势持续向好

2010 年，国民经济回升向好的基础不断巩固，国内生产总值达到 397983 亿元，超过日本成为世界第二大经济体。国内生产总值增速为 10.3%，比上年加快 1.1 个百分点。全年财政收入 83080 亿元，比上年增长 21.3%；其中税收收入 73202 亿元，比上年增长 23.0%。2010 年底国家外汇储备 28473 亿美元，比上年底增加 4481 亿美元。

改革开放取得重要进展

经济体制改革、政治体制改革以及其他各领域的改革协调推进。国有经济布局和结构战略性调整加快实施，资源性产品价格、环保收费、财税体制、财政管理体制、金融体系等重点领域和关键环节改革实现新突破，社会主义市场经济体制更加完善。与发达国家的经贸关系得到加强和改善，与发展中国家的互利合作进一步深化，对外贸易结构更加合理。全年货物进出口总额 29728 亿美元，比上年增长 34.7%。实际使用外商直接投资金额 1057 亿美元，比上年增长 17.4%。

人民生活水平不断提高

在一系列利民、惠民政策的带动下，2010 年，城镇居民人均可支配收入和农村居民人均纯收入分别实际增长 7.8% 和 10.9%，2010 年底农村贫困人口比上年底减少 909 万人。全年社会消费品零售总额 156998 亿元，实际增长 14.8%。2010 年底全国民用汽车保有量达到 9086 万辆，比上年底增长 19.3%；电话普及率达到 86.5 部 / 百人；互联网普及率达到 34.3%。国内消费需求大幅增加，消费结构持续优化升级，有力保障和改善了民生，并为国民经济长远发展奠定了坚实基础。

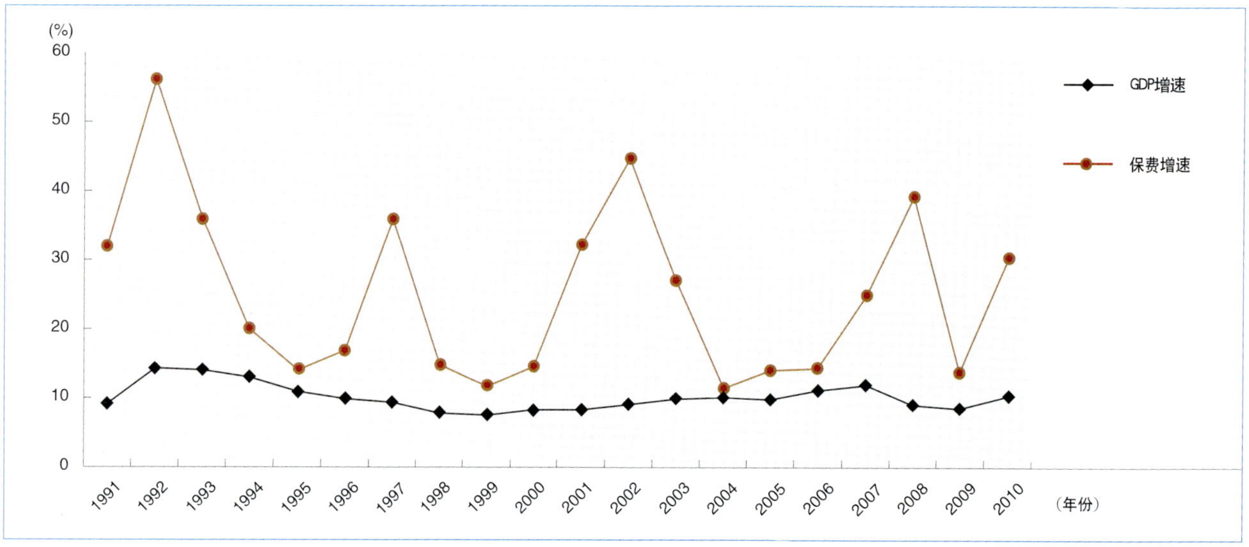

图 1　1991—2010 年 GDP 增速与保费增速对比图

金融业持续平稳健康发展，促进经济发展能力快速提升

2010 年，我国金融市场继续保持平稳健康运行，充分发挥了保证国家宏观经济政策实施、优化资源配置、推动金融体制深化改革、加大金融支持经济发展力度的积极作用。

实施适度宽松的货币政策，促进经济平稳增长

2010 年，中国人民银行继续实施适度宽松的货币政策，进一步加强流动性管理，较好地处理了保持经济平稳较快发展、调整经济结构和管理通胀预期的关系。针对经济运行的新形势、新情况，及时调整货币政策力度，按照“区别对待、有扶有控”的原则，引导金融机构加大对国家重点产业调整振兴、经济社会薄弱环节、就业、消费、节能环保、战略性新兴产业等方面的支持，严格控制对高耗能、高排放和产能过剩行业贷款。加强对系统性金融风险的监测评估，有效抑制异常外汇资金流入，切实防范跨境资金流动风险。进一步推进人民币汇率形成机制改革，人民币汇率预期总体平稳，汇率弹性明显增强。2010 年底，人民币汇率为 1 美元兑 6.6227 元人民币，比上年底升值 3%。

银行业保持稳健运行，抗风险能力明显提升

2010 年，银行业稳步推进平台贷款清理和风险化解工作，确保信贷资金进入实体机构。坚持以房为限实施差别化房贷政策，加强对房地产信托业务的监管。进一步优化信贷结构，防范产业结构调整相关风险。中国农业银行顺利完成 A+H 股公开发行上市，成为 2010 年全球融资规模最大的 IPO。截至 2010 年底，银行业金融机构资产总额 95.3 万亿元，比上年增长 19.9%，资本充足率 12.2%，核心资本充足率 10.1%。商业银行不良贷款余额和比例继续保持“双降”。其中，不良贷款余额为 4336 亿元，比上年减少 732 亿元；不良贷款率 1.13%，比上年下降 0.45 个百分点。银行业抗风险能力大幅提高，国际声誉显著提升。

资本市场平稳运行，市场体系日益完善

2010 年，我国资本市场总体平稳健康运行，功能得到较好发挥。证券市场积极推动并购重组市场化改革，融资效率不断提升。股指期货与融资融券业务试点成功推出。新股发行体制改革深化推进。截至 2010 年底，沪深股市总市值达到 26.5 万亿元，上证综合指数、深证成分指数分别收于 2808 点和 12459 点，分别比上年底下跌 14.3% 和 9.1%。股票筹资规模创历史最高水平，各类企业和金融机构在境内外股票市场上通过发行、增发、配股以及行权方式累计筹资 1.13 万亿元，同比多筹资 6351 亿元，为上年同期的 2.3 倍。债券市场发行规模稳步扩大，累计发行人民币债券 5.2 万亿元，比上年增长 5.4%。

保险市场良性发展，综合实力显著增强

2010 年，中国保险业有效巩固和扩大应对金融危机冲击成果，继续保持了良好发展势头。行业改革稳步推进，保险资金投资渠道在股权投资、不动产投资等领域进一步拓宽，多家银行参股保险公司，保险营销员体制改革正式启动。46 家保险公司增资 331.7 亿元，8 家公司发行次级债 225.5 亿元，行业偿付能力状况得到显著改善。全国实现保费 1.45 万亿元，比上年增长 30.4%。保险资金运用余额达到 4.6 万亿元，资金运用收益达 2014.6 亿元，平均收益率为 4.84%。

专栏一

国家“十二五”规划出台

2011 年 3 月 14 日，十一届全国人大四次会议表决通过《关于国民经济和社会发展第十二个五年规划纲要》。纲要全文约 6 万字，共分为 16 篇，突出了科学发展的主题和加快转变经济发展方式的主线，提出了未来五年经济社会发展的指导思想、总体思路、目标任务和重大举措，是我国经济社会发展的宏伟蓝图，是全国各族人民共同的行动纲领，是政府履行经济调节、市场监管、社会管理和公共服务职责的重要依据。

专栏二

中央出台一系列政策调控物价和房价

2010 年下半年以来，受国内外多种因素影响，以农产品为主的生活必需品及商品房价格较快上涨，通货膨胀压力不断攀升，给国民经济运行带来不稳定因素。党中央、国务院科学判断形势，综合运用多种调控手段，及时出台一系列针对性政策措施，全面加强和改进价格调控和监管，正确引导市场预期，有效抑制了价格过快上涨势头，切实保障了人民群众基本生活。

叁

保险业服务经济社会建设

- 服务和支持『三农』
- 促进经济转型升级
- 完善多层次社会保障体系
- 参与社会风险管理

2010 年，保险业深入贯彻落实科学发展观，坚持“想全局、干本行，干好本行、服务全局”，在服务经济社会发展大局中发挥了积极作用。

保险业服务经济社会建设

服务和支持“三农”

2010 年，我国农业保险覆盖面继续拓宽，承保品种由水稻、小麦等 5 类主要粮食作物扩展至林木、油菜等经济作物，保障范围由种植业、养殖业扩展至农房、农机等多个领域，地域由初期的 6 个试点省区扩大至所有省区市。中央财政补贴的品种增加到 14 个。各地政府也纷纷出台政策支持农业保险发展，推出食用菌、水产养殖、林果、天然橡胶保险等试点，有效地支持了地方特色农业发展。全年农业保险实现保费 135.9 亿元，提供风险保障 3943.1 亿元，参保农户 1.4 亿户次，承保主要粮油棉作物 6.8 亿亩，占全国播种面积的 35%；承保森林 4.8 亿亩，同比增加 68%；承保牲畜 6.3 亿头（羽、只），其中能繁母猪 2468.3 万头。全年农业保险赔款累计 96 亿元，受益农户 1979.2 万户次。

促进经济转型升级

支持产业创新发展。大力推动自主创新，积极探索科技保险、文化产业保险、环境污染责任保险等险种试点，为创新型企业提供风险保障，促进经济低碳发展、绿色发展。机电、汽车整车零部件、高新技术产品、纺织品、轻工产品、农产品及医药产品等七大重点行业承保金额增幅达 80.5%。

保障和发展内外贸易。信用保险为国内外贸易承担风险金额 24181.8 亿元，同比增长 165.3%。其中，短期出口信用险全年实现保额 1543.3 亿美元，创历史新高，同比增长 71%，超额完成国务院部署的 1200 亿美元承保任务；大型成套设备出口融资保险完成承保方案 45 个，涉及合同金额 110.1 亿美元；出口信用保险对我国一般贸易出口渗透率由 2009 年的 18.6% 提高到 22.8%。

积极拉动居民消费。大力发展消费信贷保证保险，通过住房、汽车等消费贷款保证保险，承担风险金额 2693.4 亿元。

完善多层次社会保障体系

健康保障委托管理业务取得新的突破。积极落实国家医改政策措施，参与新农合、城镇职工和居民基本医疗保险、医疗救助等经办管理，为完善医疗保障体系发挥了重要作用。其中，保险业参与医药卫生体制改革的“湛江模式”在全国受到广泛关注，在政府不增加投入、群众不增加负担的情况下，医疗保障水平大幅提高，覆盖面更加广泛。全年新增健康保障委托管理资金 89.7 亿元，为 2186.9 万人次提供赔付与补偿服务。2010 年，健康保险业务新增承保人次 8.4 亿，新增风险保障 23.9 万亿元，赔款和给付金额 264 亿元。

养老保障范围逐步扩大。截至 2010 年底，共为 729.2 万人次提供了商业养老风险保障。为 7634.6 万人次提供了年金保险服务。养老保险公司收取企业年金受托业务缴费 357.4 亿元，较年初增长 35.6%；受托管理资产 1039.1 亿元，投资管理资产 709 亿元，较年初分别增长 46.5% 和 45.9%。

参与社会风险管理

2010 年，保险业共承担各类责任风险保障金额 33.1 万亿元，支付补偿金 44 亿元。其中，分别为公众责任、产品责任、雇主责任、职业责任支付补偿金 21.3 亿元、2.7 亿元、11 亿元、6.2 亿元。

完善保险参与风险管理的机制。联合公安部在 20 个省市建立酒后驾驶与机动车交强险费率挂钩浮动机制，交强险制度进一步完善。与有关部委共同出台《道路交通事故社会救助基金管理办法》。重点推进旅行社责任、环境污染、安全生产、校方责任、医疗责任等与公众利益密切相关的责任保险发展，积极化解民事纠纷、缓解社会矛盾、维护社会稳定。

积极应对重大灾害和为重大事件提供保障。在青海玉树地震、黑龙江伊春空难、上海高层住宅火灾等重大灾害事故中，保险业积极履行赔付责任。在上海世博会、广州亚运会等重大活动中，保险业较好发挥风险保障功能，累计提供保险保障 3000 多亿元，保障人数近 500 万人次。

专栏三

保险业多种模式参与社会保障体系建设

2010 年，保险业充分发挥行业优势，积极与地方政府开展合作，参与新农合、城镇居民基本医疗保险、企事业单位社会团体补充保险等医疗保障项目，取得明显成效。覆盖人数 1.8 亿人，新增委托管理资金 89.7 亿元，实现保费 70.6 亿元，赔付与补偿 2186.8 万人次，赔付与补偿金额 109.3 亿元。在服务社会保障体系建设过程中，保险业涌现出“湛江模式”、“洛阳模式”、“晋江模式”等典型，得到社会各界的广泛好评。

专栏四

保险业积极应对重大灾害事故

2010 年，保险业按照党中央、国务院的统一部署，努力做好重大灾害事故的应对工作，在青海玉树地震、甘肃舟曲泥石流、黑龙江伊春空难、上海高层住宅火灾等重大灾害事故中，积极履行赔付责任，有效保障了人民生命财产安全和经济社会稳定运行，得到社会各界的高度认可。截至 2010 年底，在以上四次重大灾害事故中分别支付赔款 389.4 万元、1770.8 万元、2455.7 万元、904.1 万元。

肆

保险监管制度进一步完善

- 中国保险监督管理委员会职责
- 监管机构的组织框架
- 监管目标
- 监管理念日益科学完善
- 监管制度建设持续推进
- 监管力量得到充实提升
- 监管方式方法不断创新
- 市场秩序规范成效明显
- 行业风险得到有效防范

2010年，中国保监会加强监管组织体系建设，增设西藏保监局，启动监管机构延伸试点，在河北唐山、江苏苏州、浙江温州、山东烟台和广东汕头设立保险监管分局。目前，保险监管机构已覆盖全部省会城市。截至2010年底，全国保险监管工作人员共计2453人，其中保监会机关370人，派出机构2083人。

保险监管制度进一步完善

中国保险监督管理委员会职责

主要职责

1. 拟订保险业发展的方针政策，制定行业发展战略和规划；起草保险业监管的法律、法规；制定行业内规章。

2. 审批保险公司及其分支机构、保险集团公司、保险控股公司的设立；会同有关部门审批保险资产管理公司的设立；审批境外保险机构代表处的设立；审批保险代理公司、保险经纪公司、保险公估公司等中介机构及其分支机构的设立；审批境内保险机构和非保险机构在境外设立保险机构；审批保险机构的合并、分立、变更、解散，决定接管和指定接受；参与、组织保险公司的破产、清算。

3. 审查、认定各类保险机构高级管理人员的任职资格；制定保险从业人员的基本资格标准。

4. 审批关系社会公众利益的险种、依法实行强制保险的险种和新开发的人寿保险险种等保险条款和保险费费率，对其他保险险种的条款和费率实施备案管理。

5. 依法监管保险公司的偿付能力和市场行为；负责保险保障基金的管理，监管保险保证金；根据法律和国家对保险资金的运用政策，制定有关规章制度，依法对保险公司的资金运用进行监管。

6. 对政策性保险和强制保险进行业务监管；对专属自保、相互保险等组织形式和业务活动进行监管。归口管理保险行业协会、保险学会等行业社团组织。

7. 依法对保险机构和保险从业人员的不正当竞争等违法、违规行为，以及对非保险机构经营或变相经营保险业务进行调查、处罚。

8. 依法对境内保险及非保险机构在境外设立的保险机构进行监管。

9. 制定保险行业信息化标准；建立保险风险评价、预警和监控体系，跟踪分析、监测、预测保险市场运行状况，负责统一编制全国保险业的数据、报表，并按照国家有关规定予以发布。

10. 承办国务院交办的其他事项。

监管机构的组织框架

主席

副主席
副主席
副主席
副主席
纪委书记

主席助理
主席助理

办公厅
发展改革部
政策研究室
财务会计部
财产保险监管部
人身保险监管部
保险中介监管部
资金运用监管部
国际部
法规部
统计信息部
稽查局
人事教育部
监察局
机关党委

直属中国保监会的36个派出机构，根据授权履行行政管理职能，依照国家有关法律、法规和方针、政策，统一监督管理辖区内的保险市场，维护当地保险市场的合法、稳健运行，引导和促进当地保险业持续、快速、协调、健康发展。

监管目标

- 保护保单持有人利益
- 促进保险业持续、快速、协调发展
- 防范和化解风险

监管理念日益科学完善

深入落实科学发展观，坚持科学、依法、有效监管，继续转方式、调结构，持续推进保险创新，不断提高行业科学发展能力。不断健全和完善“三支柱”保险监管框架和风险防范“五道防线”。在注重防范单一保险机构风险的同时，探索推进宏观审慎监管，增强监管的前瞻性、针对性和有效性。

监管制度建设持续推进

完善公司治理和内控监管制度，提高股东准入门槛，规范公司股权流转。严格高管人员准入标准，建立高管人员轮训制度，加强对高管人员的管理和培训。加大保险业务监管力度，完善财产险公司保险条款费率管理制度，建立人身险产品动态监测制度，规范再保险业务。建立健全信息披露制度，提高保险经营透明度。全年共制定和修订《保险公司股权管理办法》、《保险集团公司管理办法》等 11 项部门规章和一系列规范性文件，并对现行监管规章制度进行了全面清理。

监管力量得到充实提升

科学布局监管机构，在西藏设立保监局，实现在内地各省、市、自治区均设有派出机构，提高了监管覆盖面。监管机构延伸取得新进展，苏州、烟台、温州、唐山和汕头 5 个监管分局挂牌成立。完善会机关内部机构设置，设立偿付能力监管部，强化专业化监管职责。通过调整充实派出机构领导班子，加大监管干部培训力度，以及加强对派出机构的巡视等措施，监管干部科学、依法和有效监管的能力和水平得到进一步提升。

监管方式方法不断创新

深入推进分类监管，建立分支机构分类监管制度，初步形成涵盖法人机构和分支机构、较为完整的分类监管体系。指导行业建立车险信息共享机制和保单承保理赔信息自主查询制度，加强被保险人利益保护工作。召开首次保险监管国际联席会议和第七次中美保险对话，加强与外资保险公司母国监管机构的监管合作。推进监管信息化建设，出台信息化工作指引和行业标准，开发偿付能力监管、信访投诉等信息管理系统，进一步强化信息化支撑与引领行业发展的能力。

市场秩序规范成效明显

围绕保护被保险人利益，加大现场检查力度，通过专项检查、重点检查、综合性检查等方式，着重开展数据不真实、理赔不规范、准备金提取不合规及销售误导、银邮代理、意外险、中介业务等检查工作。落实案件责任追究制度，共对 175 人进行问责，对涉嫌犯罪的移送司法机关。全年监管机构共派出 1949 个检查组，处罚各类保险机构 905 家次，责令撤换高管 96 人，查处商业贿赂案件 14 起，有力地维护了市场秩序。

行业风险得到有效防范

强化偿付能力监管的刚性约束，通过压力测试、偿付能力预测、监管提示等多种措施防范风险，督促部分保险公司改善偿付能力状况。截至 2010 年底，偿付能力不达标的保险公司共有 6 家，比上年减少 2 家，不达标公司偿付能力关键指标有了明显改善。出台《保险资金运用管理暂行办法》和一系列配套政策，深化保险资金运用监管。建立健全全过程的风险防控体系，推行保险公司全面风险管理。全面排查外资公司境外股东财务业务状况，切实防范国际金融风险跨境传递。

专栏五

我国召开首次保险监管国际联席会议

2010 年 12 月 6 日，中国保监会作为东道主在北京发起召开首次保险监管国际联席会议，来自法国、德国、美国等 11 个国家与地区的保险监督官出席会议。会议期间，与会各国代表分别介绍了各自监管机构应对国际金融危机的改革措施，以及在华设有营业机构的母公司运营情况，并围绕加强跨国保险集团母国监管机构之间的交流合作、共同防范跨境风险等议题深入交换了意见。

伍

保险市场运行状况

- 非寿险公司业务
- 寿险公司业务
- 专业再保险公司业务
- 保险中介市场业务
- 外资保险业务
- 保险资产管理

2010 年，中国保险业实现保费 14528 亿元，同比增长 30.4%。保险深度 3.65%[①]，同比提高 0.33 个百分点；保险密度 1083.4 元，同比提高 249 元。赔款和给付金额达 3200.4 亿元，同比增长 2.4%。保险公司总资产突破 5 万亿元，达 50467.2 亿元。全国共有保险集团公司 8 家，保险公司 125 家，比 2009 年增加 5 家，保险资产管理公司 9 家。

执行《企业会计准则解释第 2 号》后，2010 年全行业保险业务收入共计 13442.7 亿元。其中非寿险公司保险业务收入达 4058.3 亿元；寿险公司保险业务收入达 8947.3 亿元；再保险公司保险业务收入达 435.3 亿元。

保险市场运行状况

非寿险公司业务

保费持续快速增长

2010 年，在国家宏观政策的带动下，非寿险公司业务保持快速发展势头，实现保费 4026.9 亿元，同比增长 34.6%，增速比上年同期增加 12.2 个百分点，达近五年来的最高水平。

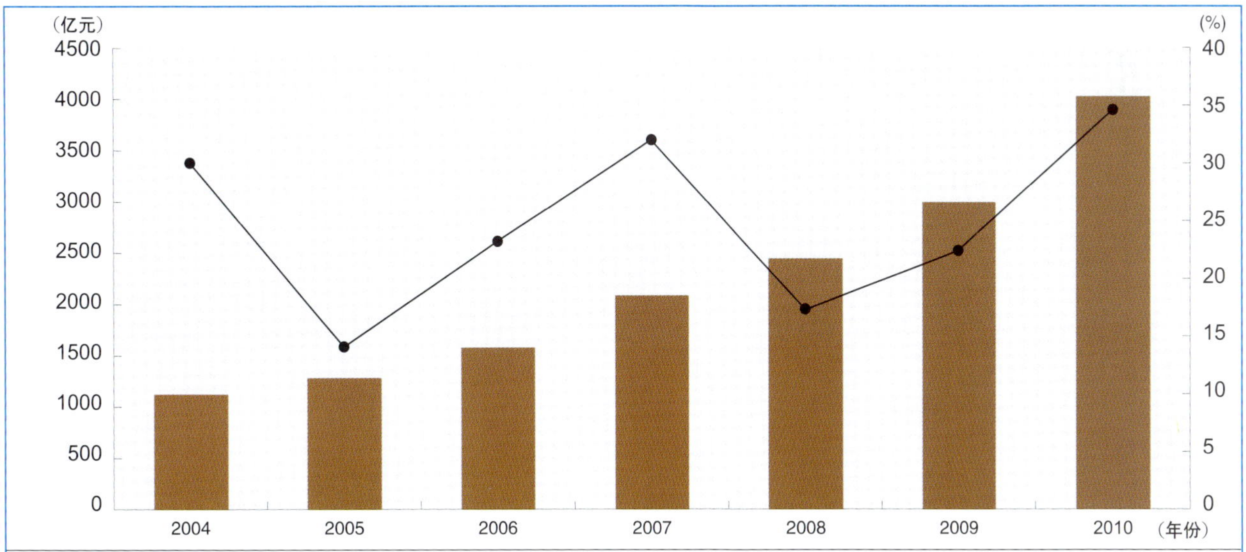

	2004	2005	2006	2007	2008	2009	2010
保费（左坐标）	1124.8	1283.5	1581.1	2086.6	2446.2	2992.9	4026.9
增速（右坐标）	30.0	14.1	23.2	32.0	17.3	22.4	34.6

图 2　2004—2010 年非寿险公司保费及增长速度

保费构成前 5 位的是车险、企财险、农业险、责任险和信用险，分别为 3004.2 亿元、271.6 亿元、135.9 亿元、115.9 亿元和 96 亿元，占非寿险公司业务的 90.0%。

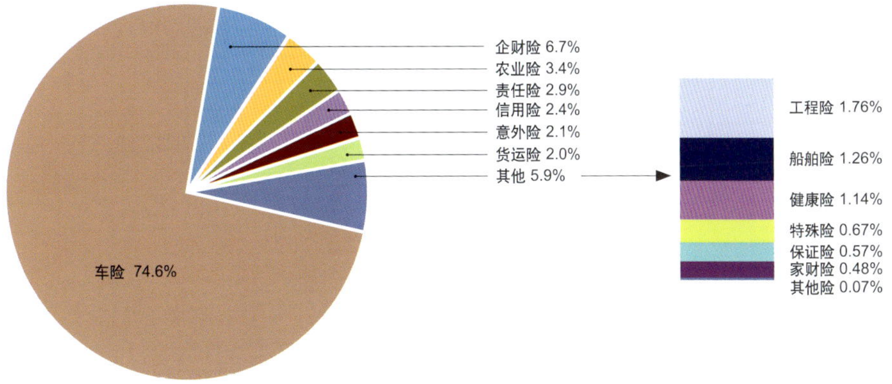

图 3　2010 年非寿险公司业务构成

① 保险深度和保险密度根据业务口径的保费数据计算得出。

非寿险多数险种继续较快增长，其中车险、企财险、责任险、信用险、货运险、工程险和船舶险业务分别增长39.4%、22.7%、25.7%、36.6%、28.5%、37.4% 和 21.5%。

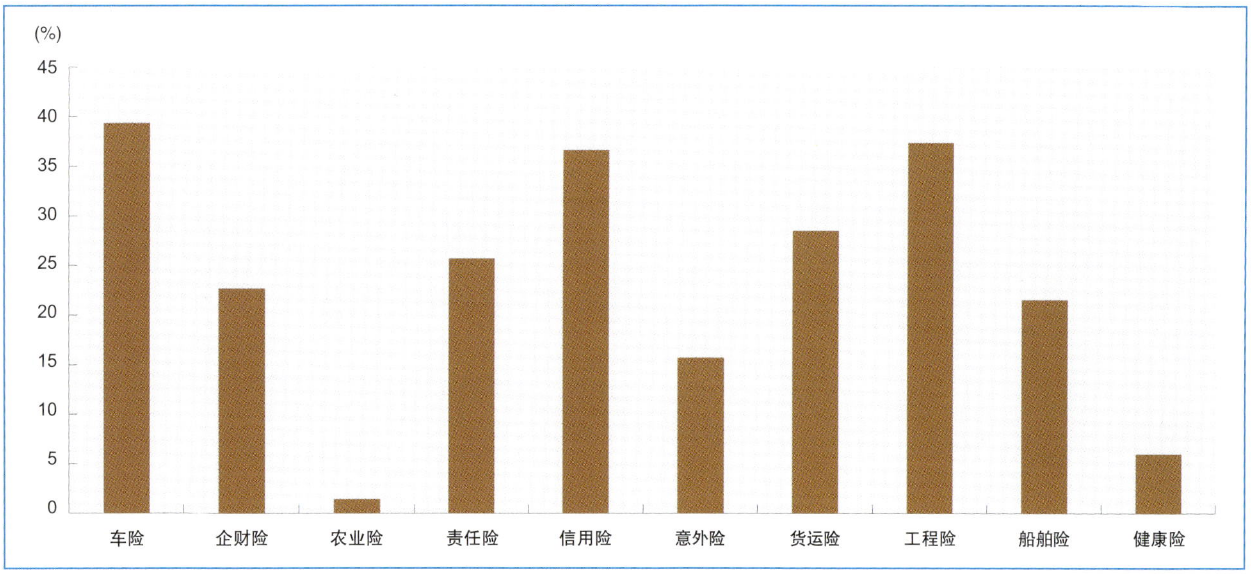

图 4　2010 年非寿险公司主要险种保费增长率

表 1　2010 年非寿险公司保费前十名

排名	名称	资本结构	保费（亿元）	市场份额（%）
1	中国人民财产保险股份有限公司	中资	1539.3	38.2
2	中国平安财产保险股份有限公司	中资	621.2	15.4
3	中国太平洋财产保险股份有限公司	中资	515.3	12.8
4	中华联合财产保险股份有限公司	中资	193.4	4.8
5	中国大地财产保险股份有限公司	中资	138.2	3.4
6	中国人寿财产保险股份有限公司	中资	112.7	2.8
7	阳光财产保险股份有限公司	中资	106.4	2.6
8	中国出口信用保险公司	中资	89.1	2.2
9	天安保险股份有限公司	中资	80.3	2.0
10	安邦财产保险股份有限公司	中资	70.3	1.8
	合计		3466.2	86.0

市场主体稳步增加，市场集中度小幅回升

截至2010年底，全国共有非寿险公司56家。其中，中资公司35家，较上年增加了泰山产险1家，外资公司21家，较上年增加了信利保险和劳合社保险①2家。

非寿险市场集中度出现小幅回升，保费前5家公司市场份额共计74.6%，较上年同期上升0.5个百分点。

赔款金额继续增长

2010年，非寿险公司赔款金额达1815.2亿元，同比增长10.8%，增速比上年同期降低0.2个百分点。其中，车险赔款金额1375.8亿元，同比增长14.6%；企财险赔款金额117.2亿元，同比下降8.1%；责任保险赔款金额44亿元，同比增长13%；货运险赔款金额28.9亿元，同比增长10.4%；农业险赔款金额96亿元，同比增长0.8%。2010年，非寿险公司已赚保费综合费用率为34.2%，较上年下降4个百分点。

承保盈利明显改善

2010年，非寿险公司承保利润为80.4亿元，承保利润率为2.56%。

专栏六

做好世博、亚运保险保障服务

2010年，中国先后迎来世博会和亚运会两项盛事。保险业认真做好保险保障服务，全程为世博会提供建筑安装工程保险、财产损失保险、展品和艺术品保险等服务，为亚运会的全部赛事活动及人员、财产提供保险服务。人保财险作为世博会和亚运会的保险合作伙伴，开发、承保了世博会、亚运会专属保险产品，制订理赔服务方案，组建保险理赔服务团队，为世博会、亚运会的顺利举办提供了有力保障。

专栏七

推进车险费率市场化改革

2010年6月，中国保监会下发《关于在深圳开展商业车险定价机制改革试点的通知》（保监产险[2010]619号），将车险价格与车辆交通违法、赔款记录等指标挂钩，开始推进商业车险定价机制改革，通过价格杠杆实现资源的合理配置，增强保险的社会管理功能。

专栏八

航运保险迎来发展契机

2010年8月9日，中国保监会批复中国人民财产保险股份有限公司和中国太平洋财产保险股份有限公司在上海试点设立"航运保险运营中心"，以积极推动航运保险市场发展，更好地服务上海"两个中心"建设。航运保险作为连接航运业和金融业的服务平台，迎来了前所未有的发展机遇。

---

① 2010年，经中国保监会批准，劳合社再保险（中国）有限公司扩展经营直接保险业务，公司性质由再保险公司变更为财产保险公司，同时更名为劳合社保险（中国）有限公司。

准备金余额继续上升

截至 2010 年底，非寿险公司未到期责任准备金和未决赔款准备金达到 3283.9 亿元，较上年增长 35.1%。其中，非寿险公司未到期责任准备金为 1760.1 亿元，未决赔款准备金为 1523.8 亿元。

2010 年，非寿险公司提取未到期责任准备金 414.7 亿元，提取未决赔款准备金 393.8 亿元。

寿险公司业务①

寿险公司保费突破 1 万亿元

2010 年，全国寿险公司实现保费 10500.9 亿元，保费规模首次突破万亿元大关，同比增长 28.9%，增速较 2009 年提高了近 18 个百分点。寿险公司保费占全国总保费的 72.3%。截至 2010 年底，寿险新单保费 6882.5 亿元，同比增长 26.8%，占寿险公司全部业务的 65.5%。其中，新单期交保费 1804.5 亿元，同比增长 32.2%，占寿险新单保费的 26.2%。

2010 年，寿险行业实现利润总额 736.3 亿元。行业整体偿付能力充足，偿付能力溢额 1453 亿元，各项风险得到进一步防范。

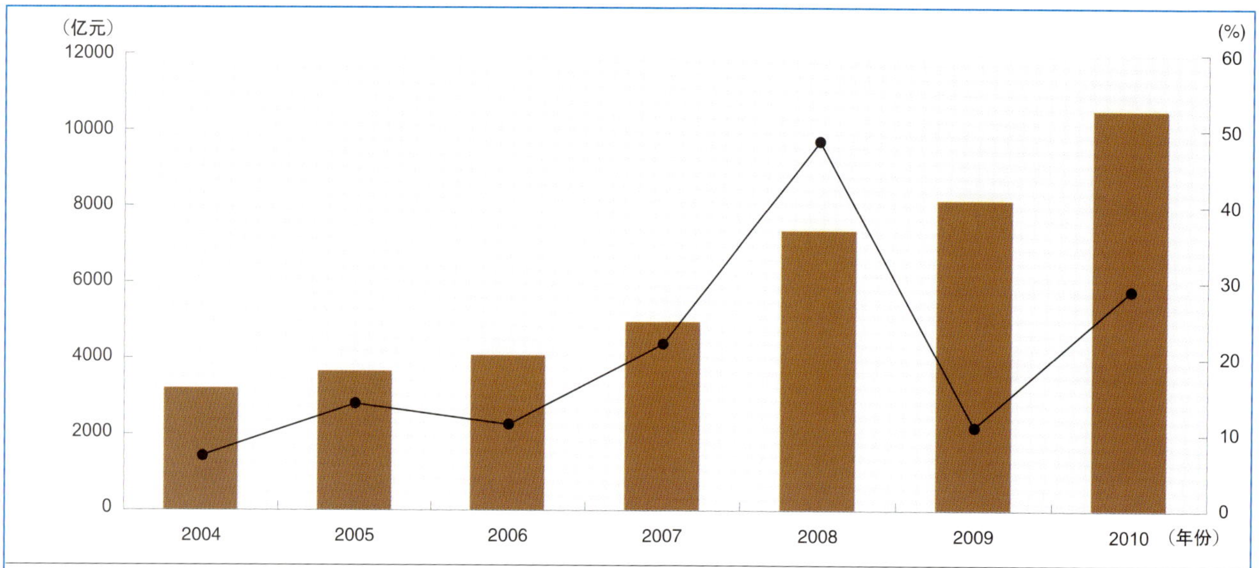

	2004	2005	2006	2007	2008	2009	2010
保费（左坐标）	3198.2	3644.9	4059.1	4946.5	7342.6	8144.2	10500.9
增速（右坐标）	7.2	14.0	11.3	21.9	48.5	11.0	28.9

图 5　2004—2010 年寿险公司保费及增长速度

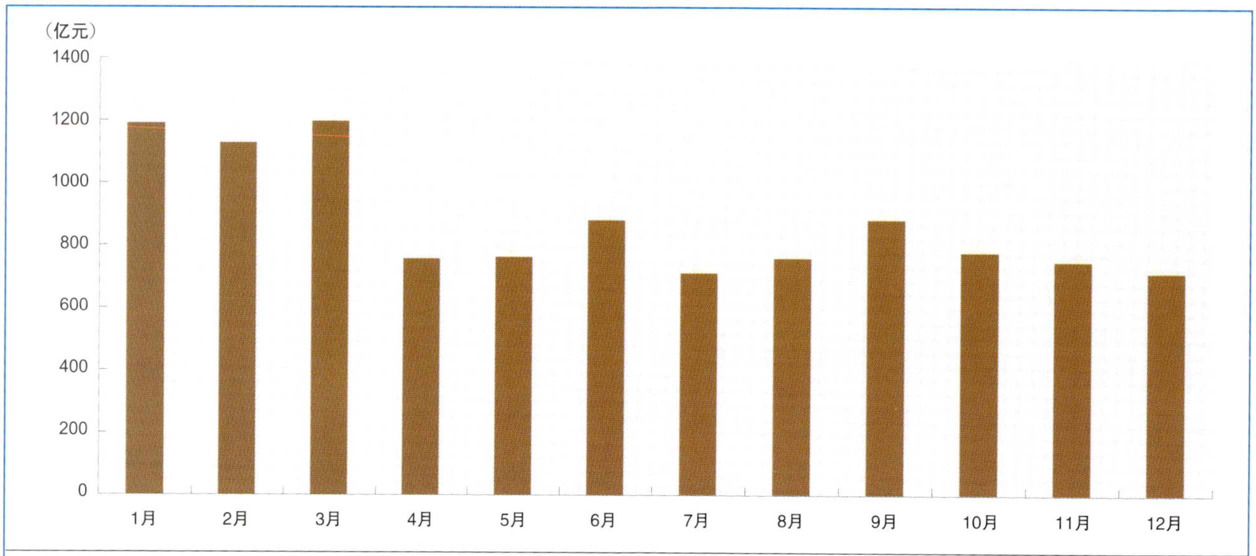

	1月	2月	3月	4月	5月	6月	7月	8月	9月	10月	11月	12月
保费	1189.6	1127.0	1196.6	756.2	761.9	879.8	711.1	758.6	881.8	777.5	748.2	712.6

图 6　2010 年寿险公司月度保费

① 含专业健康保险公司和养老保险公司。

分红险占比继续提升

2010 年，各寿险公司进一步调整产品结构，加大保障型产品营销力度。分红险在寿险保费中的占比继续提升，实现保费 7454.8 亿元，同比增长 40.9%，占寿险公司保费的 71%，占比较上年同期上升 6 个百分点。

万能险保费 1123.6 亿元，同比增长 6.5%，占寿险公司保费的 10.7%，占比下降 2.3 个百分点。投连险保费 152.8 亿元，同比增长 3.3%，占寿险公司保费的 1.5%，占比下降 0.4 个百分比。普通寿险保费 948.2 亿元，同比下降 1.4%，占寿险公司业务的 9%，占比下降 2.8 个百分点。

健康险和意外险保费合计 821.6 亿元，同比增长 19.6%，占寿险公司保费的 7.8%，同比下降 0.6 个百分点。

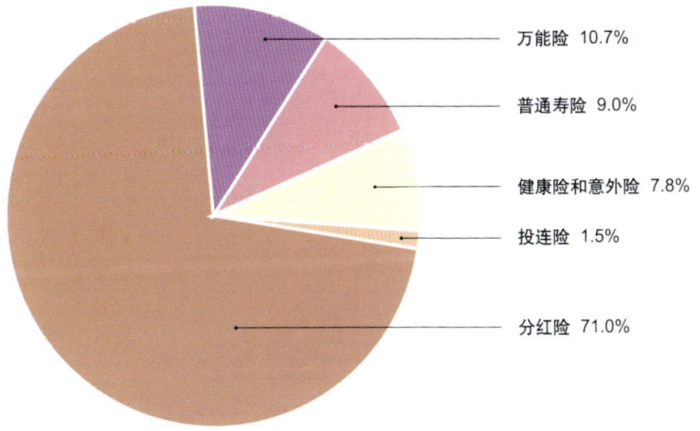

图 7　2010 年寿险公司业务构成

各渠道业务稳定发展

个人营销渠道实现保费 4314.9 亿元，同比增长 20.9%，占寿险公司业务总量的 41.1%，占比下降了 2.7 个百分点。

银行邮政代理渠道实现保费 5245.4 亿元，同比增长 35%，占寿险公司业务总量的 50%，占比上升了 2.2 个百分点。

公司直销业务实现保费 749.5 亿元，同比增长 39.1%，占寿险公司业务总量的 7.1%，占比上升了 0.5 个百分点。

专业代理渠道实现保费 62.7 亿元，同比增长 6%。保险经纪实现保费 26.7 亿元，同比增长 65.6%。

市场体系进一步优化

截至 2010 年底，全国共有 61 家人身保险公司，较上年增加两家。其中，中资公司 35 家，增加了中融人寿、安邦人寿两家公司；外资公司 26 家，较上年减少两家[①]。保费前 5 家公司市场份额共计 72.8%，较上年同期下降 4.3 个百分点。

表 2　2010 年寿险公司保费前十名

排名	名称	资本结构	保费（亿元）	市场份额（%）
1	中国人寿保险股份有限公司	中资	3330.4	31.7
2	中国平安人寿保险股份有限公司	中资	1590.6	15.2
3	新华人寿保险股份有限公司	中资	936.4	8.9
4	中国太平洋人寿保险股份有限公司	中资	920.0	8.8
5	泰康人寿保险股份有限公司	中资	867.6	8.3
6	中国人民人寿保险股份有限公司	中资	824.3	7.9
7	太平人寿保险有限公司	中资	330.2	3.1
8	生命人寿保险股份有限公司	外资	153.2	1.5
9	阳光人寿保险股份有限公司	中资	151.7	1.4
10	中国人民健康保险股份有限公司	中资	92.9	0.9
	合计		9197.3	87.7

① 2010 年，恒康天安人寿保险有限公司、光大永明人寿保险有限公司发生股权变更，由合资寿险公司变更为中资寿险公司。同时，恒康天安人寿保险有限公司更名为天安人寿保险股份有限公司。

退保率继续下降[1]

2010 年，寿险公司退保金额 1158.7 亿元，同比增长 8.3%。退保率为 3.05%，同比下降 0.48 个百分点。其中，中资寿险公司退保率为 2.96%，外资寿险公司退保率为 4.81%。

赔款与给付金额同比下降

寿险公司各项赔款与给付金额 1384.9 亿元，同比下降 6.9%。

表 3　2010 年寿险公司赔款给付金额

险种	赔款给付金额（亿元）	同比增长（%）	占比（%）
寿险	1108.7	-12.6	80.1
健康险	232.9	27.4	16.8
意外险	43.3	21.3	3.1
合计	1384.9	-6.9	100.0

专栏九

规范银行保险业务

2010 年下半年以来，中国银监会、中国保监会先后发布《关于进一步加强商业银行代理保险业务合规销售与风险管理的通知》（银监发 [2010]90 号）、《商业银行代理保险业务监管指引》（保监发 [2011]10 号）等规范性文件，围绕保护消费者权益的目标，针对银保业务经营管理的关键环节和主要风险点，从加强销售机构和人员资格管理、加强对销售行为的管控、规范银保产品和代理费用管理等方面入手，对银保市场开展全面系统的规范治理。

① 退保金及退保率为业务口径统计数据。

专业再保险公司业务

截至 2010 年底，全国共有 1 家再保险（集团）公司，即中国再保险（集团）公司；8 家专业再保险公司，即中国财产再保险股份有限公司、中国人寿再保险股份有限公司、慕尼黑再保险公司北京分公司、瑞士再保险公司北京分公司、德国通用再保险公司上海分公司、法国再保险公司北京分公司、汉诺威再保险股份公司上海分公司、太平再保险有限公司北京分公司。

2010 年，全国再保险公司的总分入保费为 435.5 亿元，同比增长 0.5%；全国再保险公司的总分保赔款金额为 172.5 亿元，同比下降 27%。

保险中介市场业务

2010 年，通过保险中介渠道实现的保费 10941.3 亿元[①]，同比增长 19.4%，占全国总保费的 75.4%。

表 4　2010 年各保险中介渠道实现保费及占比情况

销售渠道	保险代理公司	保险经纪公司	保险兼业代理机构	保险营销员	合计
保费（亿元）	481.7	313.1	5464.4	4682.1	10941.3
同比增长（%）	46.5	28.0	22.5	13.5	19.4
保费占比（%）	3.3	2.1	37.7	32.3	75.4

专业中介机构

2010 年，全国共有保险专业中介机构 2550 家，同比减少 20 家。其中，保险代理机构 1853 家，保险经纪机构 392 家，保险公估机构 305 家。

2010 年，全国保险专业中介机构实现业务收入 118.4 亿元，同比增长 32.7%；实现净利润 8.2 亿元，同比增长 71.9%。其中，保险代理公司实现佣金收入 63.1 亿元，同比增长 40.8%；实现净利润 2 亿元，同比增长 134.1%。保险经纪公司实现营业收入 44 亿元，同比增长 32.8%；实现净利润 5.7 亿元，同比增长 62.2%。保险公估公司实现业务收入 11.6 亿元，同比增长 2.7%；实现净利润 0.5 亿元，同比增长 18.4%。

兼业代理机构

截至 2010 年底，全国共有保险兼业代理机构 189877 家，同比增长 27.5%。实现佣金收入 283.5 亿元，同比增长 27.6%。

表 5　2010 年保险兼业代理渠道业务结构情况

渠道名称	机构数量（家）	数量占比（%）	保费（亿元）	保费占比（%）	佣金收入（亿元）	佣金占比（%）
银行类	113632	59.9	3503.8	64.1	149.9	52.9
邮政类	24845	13.1	896.0	16.4	34.3	12.1
铁路	435	0.2	3.1	0.1	0.4	0.1
航空	2171	1.1	7.2	0.1	4.3	1.5
车商	23859	12.6	424.8	7.8	51.8	18.3
其他	24935	13.1	629.6	11.5	42.8	15.1
合计	189877	100.0	5464.5	100.0	283.5	100.0

① 本部分数据来源于保险公司和专业保险中介机构上报保险监管部门的报表。

保险营销员

截至 2010 年底，全国共有保险营销员 329.8 万人，同比增长 13.5%。其中，寿险营销员 287.9 万人，同比增长 11.7%；产险营销员 41.9 万人，同比增长 27.4%。

外资保险业务

2010 年，外资保险公司实现保费 634.3 亿元，同比增长 38.5%，增速比上年提高 21 个百分点，占全国保费的 4.4%，比上年提高 0.3 个百分点。各类赔款与给付金额 73.7 亿元，同比增长 24.5%。

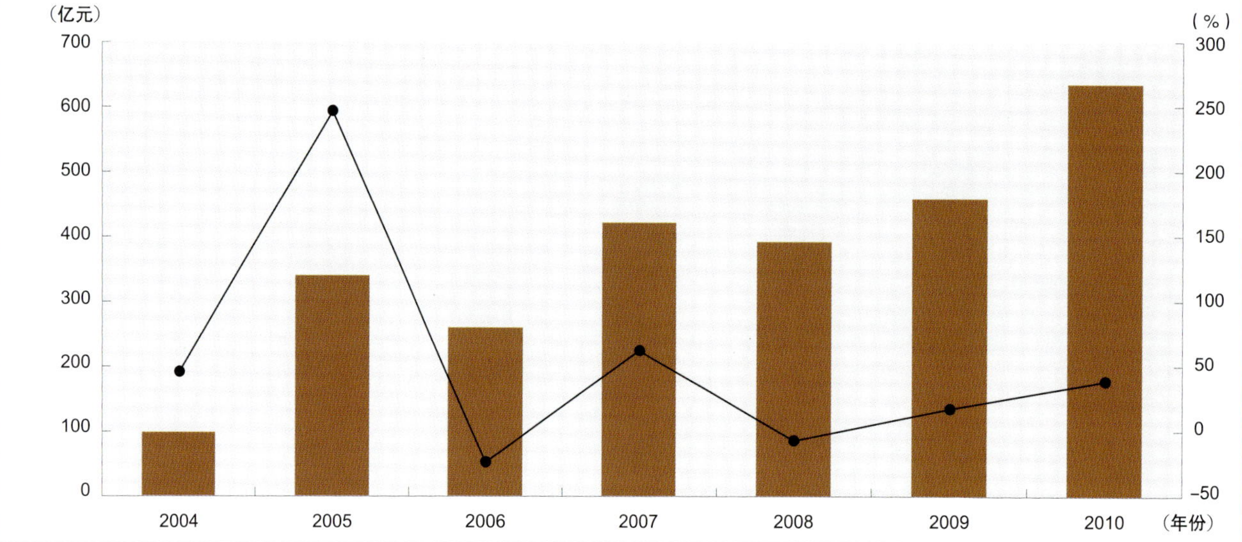

	2004	2005	2006	2007	2008	2009	2010
保费（左坐标）	97.9	339.3	259.4	420.5	391.2	458.0	634.3
增速（右坐标）	45.7	246.3	–23.5	62.1	–7.0	17.5	38.5

图 8　2004—2010 年外资保险公司保费及增长率

2010 年，外资非寿险公司实现保费 42.8 亿元，同比增长 34.9%，占全国非寿险公司保费的 1.1%。其中，货运险、企财险、责任险保费占外资非寿险公司业务的 73.2%。外资非寿险公司赔款金额 16 亿元，同比增长 38.2%；已赚保费综合费用率为 60.3%。

专栏十

开展保险公司中介业务检查

2010 年，中国保监会在全国范围内开展了保险公司中介业务检查，重点查处保险公司利用中介业务和中介渠道进行弄虚作假、虚增成本、非法套取资金等突出问题。全年共派出 44 个检查组，对 21 家保险法人的 58 个基层机构进行检查，查明保险公司非法套取资金 1.4 亿元，依法处罚保险公司及保险中介机构 117 家，吊销 1 家省级公司营业部经营保险业务许可证，罚款合计 1323 万元；处理责任人员 138 名，行业终身禁入 2 人；向司法机关移送违法犯罪线索 15 起。通过此次大检查，进一步规范了中介市场秩序，控制了潜在风险，切实保护了被保险人的利益。

专栏十一

保险营销员体制改革破冰

2010 年 10 月 21 日，中国保监会下发《关于改革完善保险营销员管理体制的意见》，明确了“稳定队伍、提升素质、创新模式”的总体思路，提出了“构建一个法律关系清晰、管理责任明确、权利义务对等、收入与业绩挂钩、基本保障健全、合法规范、渠道多元、充满活力的保险销售体系；造就一支职业品行良好、专业素质较高、可持续发展的保险营销队伍”的改革目标。启动营销员管理体制改革，对于我国保险业长期可持续健康发展、防范保险市场系统性风险、保护被保险人利益具有深远意义。

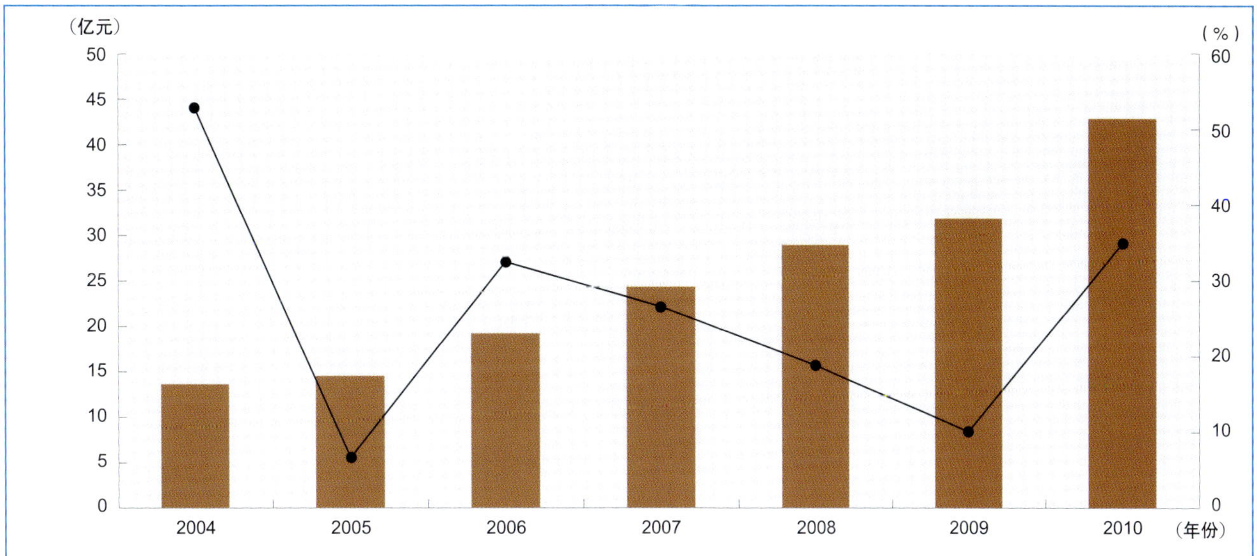

	2004	2005	2006	2007	2008	2009	2010
保费（左坐标）	13.6	14.5	19.2	24.3	28.9	31.8	42.8
增速（右坐标）	52.8	6.7	32.5	26.6	18.8	10.1	34.9

图 9　2004—2010 年外资非寿险公司保费及增长率

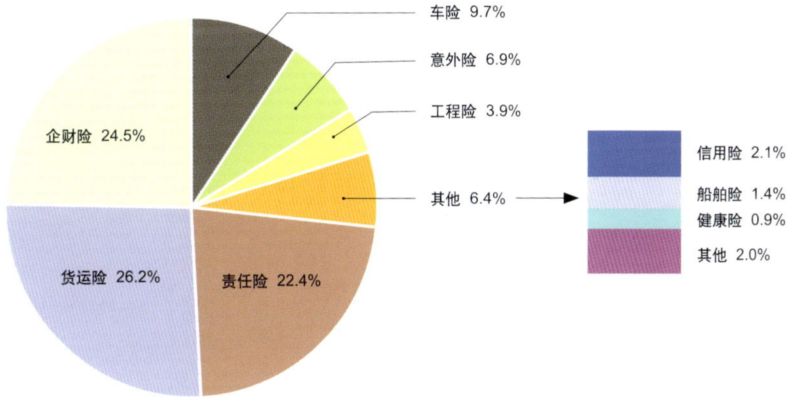

图 10　外资非寿险公司业务构成

2010 年，外资寿险公司保费为 591.5 亿元，同比增长 38.8%，占全国寿险公司保费的 5.6%。外资寿险公司赔款给付金额为 57.7 亿元，同比增长 21.3%。退保率为 4.81%。

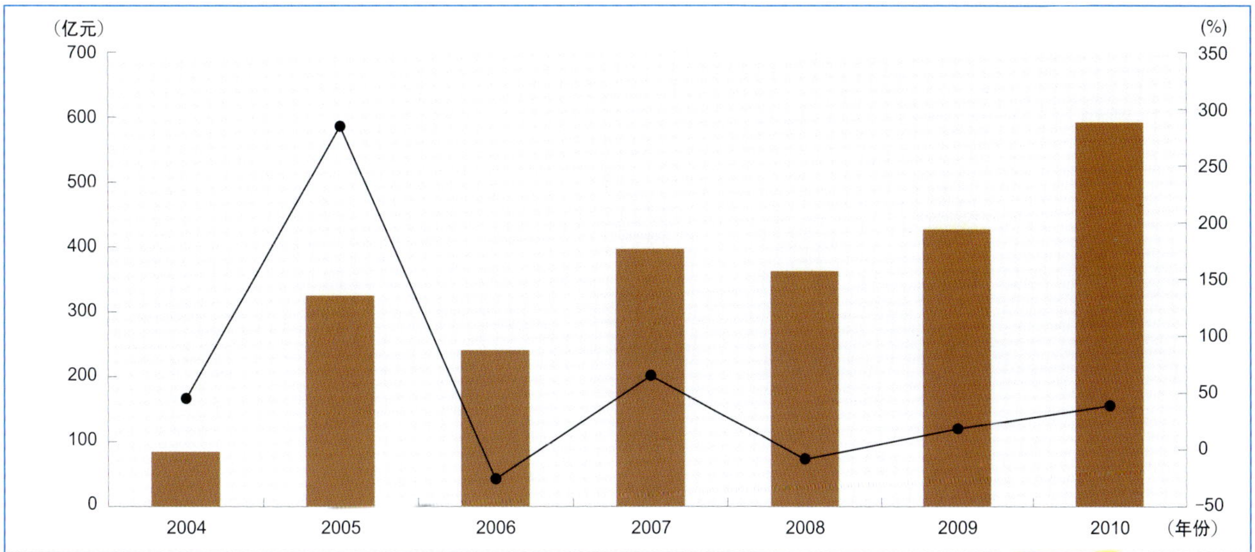

	2004	2005	2006	2007	2008	2009	2010
保费（左坐标）	84.4	324.8	240.2	396.2	362.3	426.3	591.5
增速（右坐标）	44.8	284.7	−26.0	64.9	−8.6	18.1	38.8

图 11　2004—2010 年外资寿险公司保费及增长率

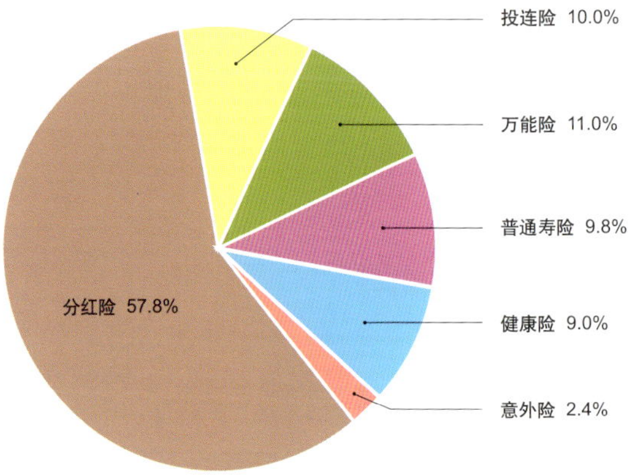

图 12　外资寿险公司业务构成

外资再保险公司分入保费为 176.8 亿元，同比增长 43%，占全国再保险公司分入保费的 40.6%。分保赔款金额为 43.8 亿元，同比减少 16.5%。

截至 2010 年底，全国共有 52 家外资保险公司，其中非寿险公司 21 家、寿险公司 26 家、再保险公司 5 家。

表 6　外资非寿险公司市场份额前五名①

序号	2010 年		2009 年	
	名称	在外资非寿险公司中占比（%）	名称	在外资非寿险公司中占比（%）
1	美亚	23.8	美亚	25.5
2	东京海上	9.7	东京海上	10.4
3	三井住友	9.5	三井住友	10.3
4	利宝互助	8.9	三星	8.3
5	三星	8.5	安联	8.1
	合计	60.4	合计	62.6

表 7　外资寿险公司市场份额前五名

序号	2010 年		2009 年	
	名称	在外资寿险公司中占比（%）	名称	在外资寿险公司中占比（%）
1	友邦	14.3	友邦	18.9
2	中意	10.4	中意	10.6
3	华泰人寿	10.3	华泰人寿	10.2
4	信诚	9.2	中英人寿	9.8
5	中英人寿	8.3	信诚	9.4
	合计	52.5	合计	58.9

2010 年，外资保险公司业务主要集中在上海、北京、广州、深圳等开放较早、发展较快的城市，上述 4 个城市外资保费合计占全国外资保费的 65.3%，比 2009 年上升 1.9 个百分点。

表 8　上海、北京、广州、深圳外资保险发展情况

城市	外资保险公司			外资非寿险公司			外资寿险公司		
	保费（亿元）	同比增长（%）	在外资公司中的占比（%）	保费（亿元）	同比增长（%）	在外资非寿险公司中的占比（%）	保费（亿元）	同比增长（%）	在外资寿险公司中的占比（%）
上海	158.6	40.5	25.0	17.5	28.7	40.9	141.1	42.2	23.9
北京	157.6	57.2	24.8	7.5	86.6	17.5	150.1	54.9	25.4
广州	69.5	29.5	11.0	6.4	27.3	15.0	63.1	29.8	10.7
深圳	28.5	23.9	4.5	2.9	25.6	6.8	25.6	23.8	4.3

① 根据各公司保费数据计算。

保险资产管理

保险资产规模快速增长

2010 年，我国继续实施应对国际金融危机的一揽子计划，国民经济运行态势进一步向好，保险行业保费持续增长，资产规模快速增加。截至 2010 年底，保险公司总资产突破 5 万亿元，达 50467.2 亿元。2010 年底，保险资金运用余额为 46046.1 亿元，较期初增长 23.1%。

保险投资收益保持稳定

全行业积极把握资本市场变化，不断优化资产配置，有效化解投资风险。全年共实现资金运用收益 2014.6 亿元，投资收益率为 4.84%。其中，利息收入 386 亿元，占资金运用收益的 19.2%；债券投资收益 943 亿元，占资金运用收益的 46.8%；证券投资基金投资收益 271.3 亿元，占资金运用收益的 13.5%；股票（股权）投资收益 353.7 亿元，占资金运用收益的 17.6%。

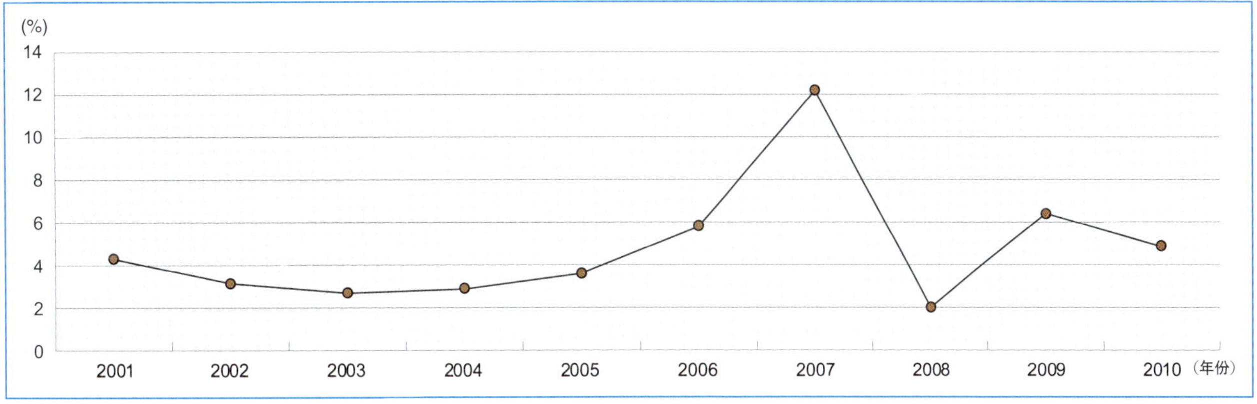

图 13　2001—2010 年保险行业资金投资收益率

保险投资渠道进一步拓宽

2010 年，保监会先后颁布《保险资金运用管理暂行办法》、《关于调整保险资金投资政策有关问题的通知》、《保险资金投资股权暂行办法》和《保险资金投资不动产暂行办法》四个重要部门规章及规范性文件，进一步拓宽了保险资金运用渠道。目前，保险投资已覆盖债券、股票、基金、股权、基础设施、房地产和境外投资等多个领域，有效拓展了保险公司资产配置的空间，同时对保险公司提升投资能力和风险管控能力也提出更高要求。

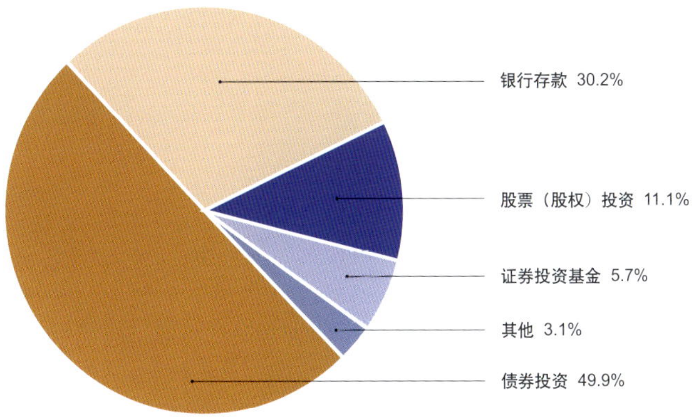

图 14　2010 年保险资金运用结构图

保险投资有效服务社会发展

保险投资加快进入与保险业务相关的养老、医疗、汽车服务等领域，有助于延伸保险服务产业链，提升保险服务的专业性与内涵。保险公司进入股权投资领域，多家保险资产管理公司发起设立基础设施债权投资计划，有效服务国民经济建设和社会发展。

陆

2011年中国保险市场发展展望

● 向好的宏观环境为保险业发展创造了广阔空间

● 转变发展方式，保险市场有望保持稳健发展

2011 年中国保险市场发展展望

向好的宏观环境为保险业发展创造了广阔空间

2011 年是“十二五”开局之年，也是经济全球化深入发展、世界经济结构加快调整、科技创新和产业转型孕育突破的一年。我国工业化、信息化、城镇化、市场化、国际化深入发展，市场需求潜力巨大，劳动力素质不断提高，基础设施日益完善，社会大局保持稳定，为保险业发展奠定了良好基础。我国将实施积极的财政政策，把货币政策从适度宽松转向稳健，继续加强和改善宏观调控，加快转变经济发展方式和调整经济结构，大力发展社会事业，扎实推进资源节约和环境保护，着力改善人民生活，全面深化改革开放，保险行业发展的空间将更为广阔。同时，我国发展面临的形势依然极其复杂，体制性矛盾和结构性问题叠加在一起，使保险业的发展面临许多不确定因素，从而对行业加强内部控制、深化结构调整、促进行业平稳较快发展提出了更高的要求。

转变发展方式，保险市场有望保持稳健发展

2011 年，中国保险业将进入快速发展期、矛盾和问题凸显期和全面转型的关键时期，机遇与挑战并存，发展与风险同在。保险行业将更加注重增强自主创新能力、提升从业人员素质、改善经营管理，加快实现从外延式发展向内涵式发展转变；更加注重培育新的业务增长点，满足经济社会发展对保险业的广泛需求，加快实现从同质化竞争向差异化竞争转变；更加注重行业可持续发展，为社会公众提供诚信、优质和高附加值的保险服务，加快实现从粗放开发资源向和谐利用资源转变。因此，随着保险业的不断努力和创新发展，中国保险市场有望保持平稳健康发展态势。

柒

附录

- 2010年中国保险市场重要监管动态
- 2003—2010年中国主要经济社会指标
- 2003—2010年中国主要金融指标
- 2003—2010年中国主要保险指标
- 中国重要经济金融网站

2010年中国保险市场重要监管动态

1.《保险机构案件责任追究指导意见》

2010年1月29日由保监会发布，自2010年7月1日起施行。主要目的是通过加大对法人机构和各级高管人员的责任追究力度，提高法人机构和管理人员的责任意识，推动保险公司主动加强内控管理，做好案件风险防控工作。

2.《保险集团公司管理办法（试行）》

2010年3月12日由保监会发布，该办法确定了保险集团公司监管的总体框架和基本内容，对保险集团公司的准入条件、公司治理、资本管理、信息披露以及监督管理作出规定，有利于进一步加强保险集团公司监管，防范保险集团经营风险，更好地促进保险业健康发展。

3.《关于金融支持文化产业振兴和发展繁荣的指导意见》

2010年3月19日由中国人民银行、中宣部、财政部、文化部、广电总局、新闻出版总署、银监会、证监会和保监会等九部委联合发布，是近年来金融支持文化产业发展繁荣的第一个宏观金融政策指导文件，对于进一步改进和提升我国文化产业金融服务、支持文化产业振兴和发展繁荣具有重要意义。

4.《保险公司股权管理办法》

2010年5月4日由保监会发布，自2010年6月10日起施行。办法进一步规范了保险公司股权流转，强化股东义务，对于加强保险公司股权监管、保持保险公司经营稳定、维护投资人和被保险人的合法权益具有重要意义。

5.《保险公司信息披露管理办法》

2010年5月12日由保监会发布，自2010年6月12日起施行。它标志着我国保险业在增强信息透明度方面迈出重要一步，有利于保障投保人、被保险人和受益人的合法权益，进一步完善保险公司治理结构，健全保险监管体系，提高保险市场运行效率，维护保险业平稳健康发展。

6.《保险公司分支机构分类监管暂行办法》

2010年5月25日由保监会发布，该办法旨在提高保监局对保险公司分支机构的监管效率，规范保监局对保险公司分支机构分类监管工作，进一步完善分类监管制度。

7.《保险资金运用管理暂行办法》

2010年7月30日由保监会发布，自2010年8月31日起施行。该办法进一步明确了保险资金运用的原则、形式、决策运行机制、风险管控和监管管理等，对规范保险资金运用行为、保障保险资金运用安全具有重要意义。

8.《保险公司内部控制基本准则》

2010年8月10日由保监会发布，自2011年1月1日起施行。准则对进一步加强保险公司内部控制建设，提高保险公司风险防范能力和经营管理水平，促进保险公司合规、稳健经营具有重要意义。

9.《保险资金投资股权暂行办法》、《保险资金投资不动产暂行办法》

2010年9月3日由保监会发布，目的是规范保险资金投资股权和不动产行为，对改善保险资产负债匹配、缓解投资压力、防范投资风险、保障资产安全具有重要意义。

10.《关于改革完善保险营销员管理体制的意见》

2010年9月20日由保监会发布，意见明确了保险营销体制改革的总体思路和总体目标，对我国保险业长期可持续健康发展、防范保险市场系统性风险、保护被保险人利益具有深远意义。

>> 附录二

2003—2010 年中国主要经济社会指标

附表 1　2003—2010 年国内生产总值及结构

年份	国内生产总值		第一产业		第二产业		第三产业	
	绝对值（亿元）	增长率（%）	绝对值（亿元）	增长率（%）	绝对值（亿元）	增长率（%）	绝对值（亿元）	增长率（%）
2003	135823	10.0	17069	2.5	62436	12.7	56318	9.5
2004	159878	10.1	20956	6.3	73904	11.1	65018	10.0
2005	182321	9.9	22718	5.2	86208	11.4	73395	9.6
2006	210871	11.1	24737	5.0	103162	13.0	82972	10.8
2007	249530	11.9	28095	3.7	121381	13.4	100054	12.6
2008	300670	9.0	34000	5.5	146183	9.3	120487	9.5
2009	335353	8.7	35477	4.2	156958	9.5	142918	8.9
2010	397983	10.3	40497	4.3	186481	12.2	171005	9.5

数据来源：历年《中国统计年鉴》和国家统计局统计公报。

附表 2　2003—2010 年底总人口、出生率及自然增长率

年份	年底总人口（万人）	出生率（‰）	自然增长率（‰）
2003	129227	12.41	6.01
2004	129988	12.29	5.87
2005	130756	12.40	5.89
2006	131448	12.09	5.28
2007	132129	12.10	5.17
2008	132802	12.14	5.08
2009	133474	12.13	5.05
2010	134100	—	—

数据来源：历年《中国统计年鉴》和国家统计局统计公报。

附表 3　2003—2010 年城镇登记失业人数及城镇登记失业率

年 份	城镇登记失业人数（万人）	城镇登记失业率（%）
2003	800	4.3
2004	827	4.2
2005	839	4.2
2006	847	4.1
2007	830	4.0
2008	886	4.2
2009	921	4.3
2010	908	4.1

数据来源：历年《中国统计年鉴》和国家统计局统计公报。

附表 4　2003—2010 年农村居民家庭人均纯收入和城镇居民家庭人均可支配收入

年份	农村居民家庭人均纯收入		城镇居民家庭人均可支配收入	
	绝对值（元）	增长率（%）	绝对值（元）	增长率（%）
2003	2622	4.3	8472	9.0
2004	2936	6.8	9422	7.7
2005	3255	6.2	10493	9.6
2006	3587	7.4	11759	10.4
2007	4140	9.5	13786	12.2
2008	4761	8.0	15781	8.4
2009	5153	8.5	17175	9.8
2010	5919	10.9	19109	7.8

数据来源：历年《中国统计年鉴》和国家统计局统计公报。

附表 5　2003—2010 年全社会固定资产投资总额

年 份	全社会固定资产投资总额（亿元）	增长率（%）
2003	55567	27.7
2004	70477	26.6
2005	88604	25.7
2006	109870	24.0
2007	137239	24.8
2008	172291	25.5
2009	224846	30.1
2010	278140	23.8

数据来源：历年《中国统计年鉴》和国家统计局统计公报。

附表 6　2003—2010 年居民消费价格指数和固定资产投资价格指数

年 份	居民消费价格指数（上年 =100）	固定资产投资价格指数（上年 =100）
2003	101.2	102.2
2004	103.9	105.6
2005	101.8	101.6
2006	101.5	101.5
2007	106.4	105.5
2008	105.9	108.9
2009	99.3	97.6
2010	103.3	103.6

数据来源：历年《中国统计年鉴》和国家统计局统计公报。

附表7　2003—2010年货物进出口总额

年份	进出口总额（亿美元）	增长率（%）
2003	8512	37.1
2004	11548	35.7
2005	14221	23.2
2006	17607	23.8
2007	21738	23.5
2008	25616	17.8
2009	22072	−13.9
2010	29728	34.7

数据来源：历年《中国统计年鉴》和国家统计局统计公报。

附表8　2003—2010年财政收支总额

年份	财政收入总额（亿元）	增长率（%）	财政支出总额（亿元）	增长率（%）
2003	21715.3	14.9	24650.0	11.8
2004	26396.5	21.6	28486.9	15.6
2005	31649.3	19.9	33930.3	19.1
2006	38760.2	22.5	40422.7	19.1
2007	51321.8	32.4	49781.4	23.2
2008	61330.4	19.5	62592.7	25.7
2009	68518.3	11.7	76299.9	21.9
2010	83080.3	21.3	89575.4	17.4

数据来源：历年《中国统计年鉴》和国家统计局统计公报。

>> 附录三

2003—2010 年中国主要金融指标

附表 1　2003—2010 年全国城乡居民人民币储蓄存款余额

年份	全国城乡居民储蓄存款余额（亿元）	年增加额（亿元）
2003	103617	16632
2004	119555	15929
2005	141051	21497
2006	161587	20544
2007	172534	10947
2008	217885	45351
2009	260772	42887
2010	303302	42530

数据来源：历年《中国统计年鉴》和国家统计局统计公报。

附表 2　2003—2010 年上市公司数量、股票发行量和股票筹资额

年份	上市公司数量（个）	股票发行量（亿股）	股票筹资额（亿元）
2003	1287	281.4	1357.8
2004	1377	227.9	1510.9
2005	1381	567.1	1882.5
2006	1434	1287.8	5594.3
2007	1550	637.2	8680.2
2008	1625	180.3	3852.2
2009	1718	400.1	4967.7
2010	2063	—	—

数据来源：历年《中国统计年鉴》和国家统计局统计公报。

附表 3　2003—2010 年黄金储备、外汇储备

年 份	黄金储备（万盎司）	外汇储备（亿美元）
2003	1929	4032.5
2004	1929	6099.3
2005	1929	8188.7
2006	1929	10663.4
2007	1929	15282.5
2008	1929	19460.3
2009	3389	23991.5
2010	3389	28473.4

数据来源：《2010 中国统计年鉴》和中国人民银行网站（www.pbc.gov.cn）。

附表 4　2003—2010 年汇率

年 份	1 美元折合人民币（期末数）	1 美元折合人民币（平均数）
2003	8.2767	8.2770
2004	8.2765	8.2768
2005	8.0702	8.1949
2006	7.8087	7.9735
2007	7.3046	7.3676
2008	6.8346	6.8424
2009	6.8282	6.8279
2010	6.6227	6.6515

数据来源：中国人民银行网站（www.pbc.gov.cn）。

>> 附录四

2003—2010 年中国主要保险指标

附表 1　2003—2010 年保费及结构

年份	保费		寿险公司		非寿险公司	
	绝对值（亿元）	增长率（%）	绝对值（亿元）	增长率（%）	绝对值（亿元）	增长率（%）
2003	3848.8	26.3	2983.2	31.1	865.6	12.0
2004	4323.0	12.3	3198.2	7.2	1124.8	30.0
2005	4928.4	14.0	3644.9	14.0	1283.1	14.1
2006	5640.2	14.4	4059.1	11.3	1581.1	23.2
2007	7033.4	25.0	4946.5	21.9	2086.6	32.0
2008	9789.1	39.2	7342.6	48.5	2446.2	17.3
2009	11137.3	13.8	8144.2	11.0	2992.9	22.4
2010	14528.0	30.4	10500.9	28.9	4026.9	34.6

附表 2　2010 年各地区保费情况

地区	保费			财产保险			人身保险		
	本年累计(万元)	同比增长(%)	占比(%)	本年累计(万元)	同比增长(%)	占比(%)	本年累计(万元)	同比增长(%)	占比(%)
全国合计	145279714.55	30.44	100.00	38956424.70	35.47	100.00	106323289.85	28.70	100.00
一、集团、总公司本级	426161.11	66.09	0.29	415787.55	71.59	1.07	10373.56	-63.05	0.01
二、东部地区	85075461.50	30.53	58.56	23259641.22	34.14	59.71	61815820.28	29.22	58.14
北京	9664550.65	38.54	6.65	2123030.12	29.12	5.45	7541520.53	41.45	7.09
天津	2140074.43	41.46	1.47	651335.45	42.23	1.67	1488738.98	41.12	1.40
河北	7464041.36	24.18	5.14	1929059.18	49.92	4.95	5534982.18	17.16	5.21
辽宁	4538131.73	31.35	3.12	1185761.26	37.13	3.04	3352370.47	29.42	3.15
大连	1510482.50	29.84	1.04	435649.33	32.50	1.12	1074833.17	28.80	1.01
上海	8838593.40	32.91	6.08	1892201.38	24.65	4.86	6946392.02	35.35	6.53
江苏	11626736.02	28.09	8.00	3119064.97	36.57	8.01	8507671.05	25.23	8.00
浙江	6903428.92	28.29	4.75	2594736.65	32.16	6.66	4308692.27	26.07	4.05
宁波	1440614.77	34.08	0.99	661979.99	29.60	1.70	778634.78	38.14	0.73
福建	3460657.01	27.11	2.38	998918.00	37.46	2.56	2461739.01	23.34	2.32
厦门	775466.53	32.80	0.53	282012.95	45.25	0.72	493453.58	26.60	0.46
山东	8762161.50	29.32	6.03	2415716.12	39.09	6.20	6346445.38	25.95	5.97
青岛	1538525.65	33.43	1.06	495450.84	44.29	1.27	1043074.81	28.82	0.98
广东	12317606.32	28.37	8.48	3090578.26	29.26	7.93	9227028.06	28.07	8.68
深圳	3614914.96	33.10	2.49	1205660.56	24.21	3.09	2409254.40	38.05	2.27
海南	479475.77	44.99	0.33	178486.17	50.58	0.46	300989.60	41.87	0.28

附表 7　2010 年代理收入前十名的保险代理公司

排名	名称	业务收入（万元）	市场份额（%）
1	华康保险代理有限公司	45176.6	7.2
2	大童保险销售服务有限公司	20496.5	3.3
3	河北盛安保险代理有限公司	12473.9	2.0
4	广东泛华南枫保险代理有限公司	10659.5	1.7
5	四川泛华保险代理有限公司	9567.6	1.5
6	东莞市南枫佳誉保险代理有限公司	7891.9	1.3
7	四川泰源保险代理有限公司	7534.7	1.2
8	河北泛联保险代理有限公司	7434.7	1.2
9	广州市泛华益安保险代理有限公司	7219.0	1.1
10	广州辉信保险代理有限公司	5032.1	0.8

附表 8　2010 年营业收入前十名的保险公估机构

排名	名称	业务收入（万元）	市场份额（%）
1	民太安保险公估股份有限公司	21244.3	18.2
2	泛华保险公估有限公司	13927.8	12.0
3	深圳市联胜保险公估有限公司	4454.3	3.8
4	上海恒量保险公估有限公司	4168.5	3.6
5	深圳市智信达保险公估有限公司	4003.5	3.4
6	根宁翰保险公估（中国）有限公司	3739.0	3.2
7	上海泛华天衡保险公估有限公司	3458.4	3.0
8	北京华泰保险公估有限公司	2554.1	2.2
9	广东衡量行保险公估有限公司	2352.3	2.0
10	广州市汇中保险公估有限公司	2159.1	1.9

>> 附录五

中国重要经济金融网站

中国人民银行：http://www.pbc.gov.cn
中国银监会：http://www.cbrc.gov.cn
中国证监会：http://www.csrc.gov.cn
中国保监会：http://www.circ.gov.cn

国家发展和改革委员会：http://www.ndrc.gov.cn
财政部：http://www.mof.gov.cn
人力资源和社会保障部：http://www.mohrss.gov.cn
国家统计局：http://www.stats.gov.cn

ANNUAL REPORT OF CHINA INSURANCE MARKET 2010-2011

2010—2011 中 国 保 险 市 场 年 报

01

Chairman's Address

In 2010, under the correct leadership of the Communist Party of China (CPC) Central Committee and State Council, China Insurance Regulatory Commission (CIRC) thoroughly applied the scientific outlook on development and, within a complex and changeable external environment, seized opportunities by focusing on the guideline of "shifting mode of growth, adjusting structures, preventing risks and promoting development". While effectively strengthening and expanding the accomplishments made in combating the global financial crisis, the CIRC also worked to accelerate the transformation of the development mode, to advance scientific, lawful and effective regulation, to prevent risks and to serve and secure the people's livelihood with the aim of providing comprehensive support for the role played by insurance. The insurance market thus maintained a good momentum of growth.

Continuous Expansion of the Insurance Market Scale

In 2010, the insurance industry realized a premium income of RMB 1452.8 billion① (+30.4% growth year-on-year (YoY)). The property and casualty insurance business continued to grow fast and the premium income totaled RMB 389.56 billion (+35.5% YoY); the personal insurance premium exceeded RMB 1.00 trillion and amounted to RMB 1063.23 billion (+28.7% YoY). The full-year compensation stood at RMB 320.04 billion. The insurance industry boasted visibly improved overall capabilities. By the end of 2010, the total assets of insurance companies also exceeded RMB 5.00 trillion and amounted to RMB 5046.72 billion; net assets reached RMB 520.89 billion, an increase of RMB 60.41 billion YoY. The utilization balance of insurance funds was RMB 4.6 trillion. Following the significant rise in the economic benefits, insurance companies made a total profit of RMB 91.03 billion, up RMB 6.53 billion YoY. The whole industry registered an investment return of RMB 201.46 billion, and the ROI was 4.84%. The reinsurance business now offers much better services.

Accelerating the Shift in the Mode of In-Surance Growth

In 2010, the insurance industry accelerated the shift in the mode of growth and continued to improve the capabilities for scientific development. It focused more on coordinated and sustained development in guiding ideology and business goals, on the match between underwriting and investment, and on harmonizing business expansion and internal management with regard to growth strategies and profitability modes. It also put more focus on quality and benefits orientation, as well as rational operation and intensive management in assessment indicators and cost policies. The entire industry continued to move the restructuring process forward and made every effort to enhance the quality of development. By improving the assessment indica-

① Unless otherwise specified, the financial data in the annual report are all the audited data based on the implementation of *the Interpretation No. 2 of the Accounting Standards for Business Enterprises*. The premium and compensation payment charges are all the data based on the business statistical approach.

tor system and relaxing the restrictive role of solvency, it promoted the growth of risk protection businesses with high inherent values. Investment-linked non-life insurance businesses continued to decline steadily, while residential property insurance and engineering insurance developed fast, up 27.5% and 37.4% YoY respectively. Traditional businesses like health and endowment insurance featuring a high degree of securing function received increasing attention; bank insurance activities continued to shift to installment premium businesses, and the installment premium of new life insurance policies grew by 32.2% YoY. The whole industry increased its innovation efforts for both products and services, developing more than 9800 new products. While giving further freedom to the advantages offered by traditional sales channels, telemarketing grew rapidly. Emerging sales modes, such as online sales catering for the habits of young consumers, saw a level of expansion that helped form a favorable landscape in which different channels complemented each other to ensure optimum development. Currently, the effort in shifting the industrial growth mode has produced initial results; the vehicle insurance business achieved positive results, and inherent values of the life insurance business have improved continuously.

Effectively Preventing and Reducing Risks

In 2010, the insurance industry took vigorous measures to prevent and reduce risks and maintain the safe and sound operation of the insurance market. Some insurance companies improved solvency by increasing the capital funds through diverse methods. In 2010, forty-six insurance companies raised RMB 33.17 billion of capital, and eight issued RMB 22.55 billion of subordinate debts. By the end of 2010, the insurance companies which could not meet the solvency standards numbered six, two fewer than in early 2010, and the key indicators of the unqualified companies saw a marked improvement. Through formulating interim measures on the utilization and management of insurance funds and relevant systems, utilization of insurance funds was regulated and the safe and sound operation of insurance funds was secured. *The Basic Rules for the Internal Control of Insurance Companies* were released to help insurance companies accelerate the establishment and improvement of internal control management systems, formulate internal control standards and processes, and make clear the responsibilities and division of labor among the boards of directors, management and internal control management departments. Dynamic solvency stress test and cash flow monitoring systems were improved along with the risk identification and early warning system. Comprehensive risk management was popularized in insurance companies, and the emergency response mechanism intended for risk prevention was further optimized. Insurance companies were encouraged to set up case accountability systems and to more significantly prevent case risks. The role of the insurance security fund was further highlighted by imparting risk treatment and remedy systems into the companies experiencing high risks. Through dispatching regulation work groups and advancing reorganization of companies, the risks facing individual companies were properly handled.

Intensifying and Improving Insurance Regulation

In 2010, the insurance regulation authority strove to advance scientific, lawful and effective regulation in order to promote the fast and sound development of the whole industry. The regulation system was successfully improved, while 11 departmental rules and a series of documents aimed at regulation were formulated through revision of the previous rules. Insurance companies were urged to be more conscious and active with regard to compliance through regulation in three categories: *legal persons, senior management* and *accountability*. Efforts were also made to improve the regulation of the organizational system, intensify information-based regulation means, upgrade regulation based on classification of legal entities, establish the regulation system based on classification of branches, explore prudent macro-regulation and strengthen the cooperation and exchanges with the regulators of the parent companies of foreign-funded insurance companies in China. Through special inspections, key inspections and comprehensive inspections, the insurance market orders were further regulated. The requirements regarding information disclosure by insurance companies were further defined, while insurance service standards and public claim handling procedure systems were established and improved. Telemarketing standards were devised. The vehicle insurance sharing mechanism and the system for self-inquiry of policy underwriting and claim information were all set up under guidance to protect the interests of the insured.

Effectively Serving Economic and Social Development

In 2010, centering on the economic construction and social development of the state, the insurance industry worked to broaden insurance coverage and improve service abilities based on securing and serving the people's livelihood. Rural households covered by agricultural insurance amounted to 140 million homes (+5.2% YoY), and RMB 394.31 billion of risk protection was offered (+3.4% YoY); the categories and coverage of insurance were further widened and the regions covered expanded to all the provinces, autonomous regions and municipalities directly under the State Council. Pilot micro-insurance programs in rural areas were broadened to 24 provinces, with the number of participants exceeding 20 million. Export credit insurance offered a risk protection more than RMB 1 trillion (+66.8% YoY) and supported an export amount comprising 22.8% of China's total general exports. Insurance companies actively participated in social risk management, realizing a liability insurance premium income of RMB 11.59 billion (+25.7% YoY). During major disasters and accidents, such as the Yushu earthquake in Qinghai province, the Yichun air crash in Heilongjiang province, and the high-rise building fire in Shanghai, the insurance industry actively fulfilled its compensation responsibility. During major events like Shanghai World Expo and Guangzhou Asian Games, the insurance industry played a fundamental role in the risk guarantee sector, offering risk protection of over RMB 300 billion and covering nearly five million individuals on a cumulative basis. The insurance companies also vigorously participated in the construction of the social security system, pushed for the specialized operation of commercial endowment and health insurance, improved product innovation and enhanced the services related to endowment and health insurance.

The achievements that the insurance industry reached in the face of the severe impact caused by the global financial crisis and the profound changes in both foreign and domestic environment in 2010 did not come easy. I would like to take this opportunity to express our sincere appreciation on behalf of China Insurance Regulatory Commission to the entire cadre of workers inside the insurance industry, to people from all walks of life, and to friends from home and abroad who have always shown an interest in and supported the reform and development of the Chinese insurance industry.

2011 is the first year of the 12th Five-year Plan period. The insurance industry will follow the spirit of the Fifth Plenum of the 17th Central Committee of CPC and the Central Economic Work Conference, further implement the scientific outlook on development and correctly tackle the new situations facing the industry. With scientific development as the theme, it will highlight the accelerated transformation of the growth pattern and adhere to lawful, scientific and effective regulation while working to prevent and dissolve insurance risks, regulate insurance market orders and protect the interests of the insured with a view to promoting its fast and steady development and making greater contributions to the construction of both a harmonious socialist society and an affluent society.

WU Dingfu
Chairman, China Insurance Regulatory Commission
May 20, 2011

02

Progress and Development of Economy and Society

- New Advances in China's Economy and Society Helped Create Space for the Development of Insurance Industry
- Further Improved Overall National Strength of China Helped Consolidate the Insurance Market Development
- Continued Fast and Sound Growth of the Financial Industry Helped Enhance the Economic Development Capacity

In the face of an extremely complex economic environment both at home and abroad and the challenges posed by severe natural disasters in 2010, China introduced a stimulus package aimed at tackling the financial crisis and worked to speed up the transformation of the economic growth mode. This innovation helped the consolidation of the upward momentum of economic and social growth and the successful completion of the 11th Five-year Plan period, thus laying the foundations for the 12th Five-year Plan period.

Progress and Development of Economy and Society

New Advances in China's Economy and Society Helped Create Space for the Development of Insurance Industry

In 2010, China conquered major natural disasters such as the Yushu earthquake in Qinghai Province and the Zhouqu mudslide in Gansu Province. The nation successfully hosted the World Expo 2010 Shanghai and Guangzhou Asian Games and fulfilled all the major objectives and tasks specified in the 11th Five-year Plan. Significant headway was made in the construction of a socialist, political, economical, cultural, social and ecological civilization.

Strengthened Foundation for the Development of Agriculture and Rural Areas

The policies drawn up for benefiting farmers were further intensified, centering on stabilizing grain production to ensure a sufficient supply, increasing farmers' income for a better livelihood, accelerating reforms for overall development and strengthening their basis for positive momentum. In 2010, the central government spent RMB 857.97 billion on issues related to agriculture, farmers and rural areas (+18.3% YoY). Direct subsidies for grain producers continued operating, while general subsidies for purchasing agricultural supplies and subsidies for purchasing superior crop varieties and agricultural machinery and tools were also provided. The minimum purchase prices for key grain products were further raised to provide farmers with additional benefits. The agricultural product processing industry was vigorously developed to further the ties between production and markets. Construction of agricultural infrastructure was strengthened, with agricultural water conservation being the prime focus. The popularization of scientific and technological innovation in the field of agriculture was accelerated, with focus being given to promoting superior varieties. The role of urban areas in assisting the development of rural regions was given further room to promote the sound interaction between urbanization and new rural developments. A new round of rural power grid upgrading was initiated and another 61.86 million rural people were provided with safe drinking water; the construction of farmers' production and living facilities was sped up. In 2010, China's grain production saw its seventh consecutive annual increase, and farmers' income continued to grow fast. Rural comprehensive reform advanced steadily. Further progress was made in both rural livelihood and rural economy, laying solid foundations to secure economic growth, the livelihood of the people and social stability.

Vigorous Advances in Economic Restructuring

China's economic performance was generally steady and the quality improved remarkably in 2010. Primary, secondary and tertiary industry grew by 4.3%, 12.2% and 9.5%, respectively. China further implemented its plan for restructuring and revitalizing key industries, comprehensively elimintating backward production facilities and making major progress in industrial restructuring. It introduced projects related to knowledge and technological innovation, and made breakthroughs in a number of cutting-edge technologies, core technologies and key equipment technologies urgently needed in industrial development. Many achievements in the field of science and technology underwent industrialization, while strategic emerging industries saw rapid growth with significantly enhanced independent innovation capabilities. Infrastructure systems and basic industries optimized their service capabilities and coordination among regional development bodies improved. Energy conservation and the reduction of emissions, ecological development and environmental protection also improved. With the accelerated shift in the growth mode and the upgrading of economic structures, new risks are emerging and more requirements are imposed on the insurance industry as the "economic propeller" and "social stabilizer".

Remarkable Achievements in Enhancing the People's Livelihood

In 2010, China maintained coordinated growth of the economy and society and aimed at achieving development centered on improving the livelihood of society as whole. Besides greater effort in implementing employment policies and advancing the reform in the medical care system, China also worked to accelerate popularization of the national tuition assistance system, to strengthen real estate regulation and to promote the development of various social undertakings related to the livelihood of the people. 2010 thus marked the best year in employment since the global financial crisis. The total number of full-year urban employees increased to 11.68 million; the registered unemployment rate in urban areas was 4.1% at the end of the year and the number of nationwide rural workers rose by 5.4% YoY. In 2010, the central finance ministry spent RMB 254.73 billion, RMB 148.54 billion, RMB 378.5 billion and RMB 112.57 billion respectively on education, medical care, social security and employment, and housing, up 28.6%, 16.7%, 14.8% and 15% YoY respectively.

Increasing Improvements of the Social Security System

The quality of the social security system continued to improve and the social security coverage expanded further. At the end of 2010, the number of people in urban areas and covered by the basic pension system was 256.73 million, 21.23 million more than the previous year. Urban inhabitants covered by basic medical insurance numbered 432.06 million, 30.59 million more than that of the previous year. The coverage of the new rural cooperative medical system widened further, with the rate of participation increasing to 96.3%. The medical funds registered a total expenditure of RMB 83.20 billion, cumulatively benefiting 700 million individuals. The number of people covered by the new rural social endowment insurance in nationwide pilot areas was 102.77 million. The criteria improved for various social assistance packages, such as minimum living allowances, minimum wages, unemployment insurance, basic pension, subsidies for objects of special care and subsidies for students from families with economic difficulties; the focus of social security shifted from an increase in quantity to both raising the quantity and improving the quality.

Further Improved Overall National Strength of China Helped Consolidate the Insurance Market Development

A Continued Upward Trend in China's National Economic Situation

In 2010, the foundations for the recovery of China's economy were consolidated further. GDP reached RMB 39798.3 billion, putting China ahead of Japan to become the world's second economy. GDP growth was 10.3%, 1.1 percentage points higher YoY. The full-year fiscal revenue totaled RMB 8308 billion (+21.3% YoY), including RMB 7320.2 billion of tax revenue (+23.0% YoY). At the end of 2010, China's foreign exchange reserves amounted to USD 2847.3 billion, USD 448.1 billion more than the previous year.

Significant Progress in Reform and Opening-up

The reforms in the economic system, the political system and other fields advanced in a coordinated manner. Implementation of national economic layout and strategic restructuring accelerated. New breakthroughs were achieved in the reforms in key fields like resource product prices, environmental protection charges, the fiscal and tax system, the fiscal administration system and the financial system. The socialist market economy system was optimized further. Economic and trade relations with developed countries were strengthened and improved, while mutually beneficial cooperation with developing countries was further deepened, resulting in a more reasonable foreign trade structure. The total trade value of imports and exports amounted to USD 2972.8 billion (+34.7% YoY). Actually utilized foreign direct investment amounted to USD 105.7 billion (+17.4% YoY).

Further Improvement of the People's Standard of Living

Fueled by a policy package aimed at benefiting the people, the per capita disposable income of urban residents and the per capita net income of rural residents respectively registered an actual growth of 7.8% and 10.9% in 2010. At the end of the year, the number of poverty-stricken rural people decreased by 9.09 million compared with the previous year. The full-year retail sales of consumer goods totaled RMB 15699.8 billion, with an actual growth of 14.8% YoY. At the end of the year, the number of private cars in the entire nation reached 90.86 million (+19.3% YoY). Telephone penetration stood at 86.5 sets per 100 people, and Internet penetration reached 34.3%. Domestic consumption demand expanded substantially with a continuous upgrade of the consumption structure, powerfully securing and improving the people's livelihood and paving the way for the long-term development of the national economy.

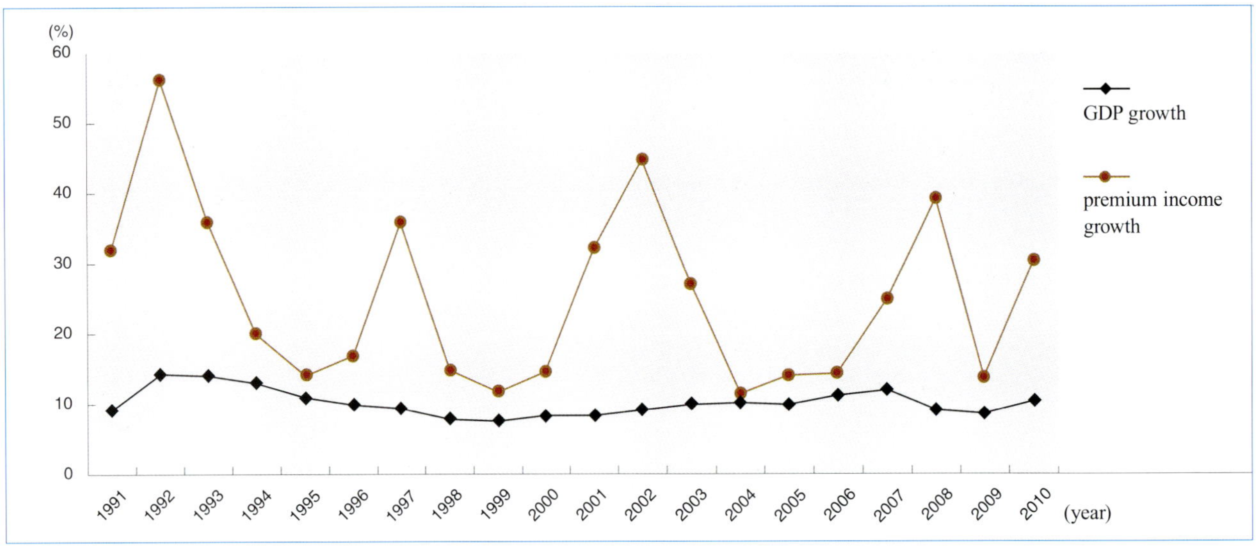

Figure 1 Comparison between GDP Growth and Annual Premium Income Growth from 1991 to 2010

Continued Fast and Sound Growth of the Financial Industry Helped Enhance the Economic Development Capacity

In 2010, China's financial market maintained steady and healthy operation and maximized its positive role in securing the implementation of China's macroeconomic policies, the optimization of resource allocation and the advancement of the financial system reform and in supporting economic development.

Moderately Relaxed Monetary Policies Promoted Steady Economic Growth

In 2010, the People's Bank of China, China's central bank, continued to implement moderately relaxed monetary policies; it intensified liquidity management further and better handled the relations between maintaining fast and steady economic development, adjusting economic structures and managing inflationary expectation. Monetary policies were adjusted in a timely manner based on the new conditions prevailing in the economy. Under the principle of "differentiated treatment and combination of both support and control", financial institutions were instructed to give support to the state's key industries during restructuring and revitalization, the weak parts of the economy and society, the fields related to employment, consumption and energy conservation and environmental protection, as well as to strategic emerging industries, and to strictly control loans granted to the industries with high energy consumption, high emissions and excess capacities. The monitoring and assessment of systematic financial risks were strengthened to effectively curb the inflow of abnormal foreign currencies and prevent risks from cross-border fund flows. The reform in the RMB exchange rate formation mechanism was further advanced, leading to generally steady RMB exchange rate expectations and clearly improved exchange rate elasticity. At the end of 2010, the RMB/USD exchange rate was RMB 6.6227 (+3% YoY).

Banking Industry Remained Stable with Increasingly Stronger Risk Resistance Capability

In 2010, the banking industry steadily controlled the work related to platform loan clean-up and risk reduction to ensure the inflow of credit funds into entities. Implementation of the differentiated housing credit policies with the number of houses being at the limit was continued, and regulation of real estate trust businesses was intensified. The credit structure was further optimized to prevent risks arising from industrial restructuring. The Agricultural Bank of China was successfully listed in A+H share markets and boasted the world's biggest IPO scale in 2010. By the end of 2010, the banking financial institutions posted a total asset of RMB 95.3 trillion (+19.9% YoY). The capital adequacy ratio was 12.2% and the core capital adequacy ratio was 10.1%. Both the balance and proportion of non-performing loans in commercial banks continued to decline. In precise terms, the balance of non-performing loans stood at RMB 433.6 billion, RMB 73.2 billion less than the previous year; the rate of non-performing loans was 1.13%, 0.45 percentage point lower compared to the year before. The banking industry enjoyed a significantly improved risk-resistance capability and a noticeably enhanced international reputation.

The Capital Market Saw Steady Operation and the Market System Became Increasingly Improved

In 2010, China's capital market saw a generally sound development and its functions were more visible. The securities market saw great advances in marketization dominated by M&A and continuously improved financing efficiency. Pilot projects of stock index futures and securities loans were successfully launched. The reform in the new stock issuance system was further deepened. By the end of 2010, Shanghai and Shenzhen stock exchanges reported a combined market value of RMB 26.5 trillion, Shanghai Composite Index and Shenzhen Component Index respectively closed down 14.3% and 9.1% YoY at 2808 points and 12459 points. The scale of fundraising through the stock market hit an historical high as various types of enterprises and financial institutions raised RMB 1.13 trillion on a cumulative basis through share offering, subsequent offering, allotment and right exercise in both domestic and foreign stock markets, up RMB 635.1 billion YoY and 2.3 times that of the same period of 2009. The bond market saw steady expansion in the issuance scale, with RMB 5.2 trillion of RMB bonds issued on a cumulative basis in 2010 (+5.4% YoY).

The Insurance Market Enjoyed Sound Development with Remarkably Improved Comprehensive Capabilities

In 2010, China's insurance industry effectively consolidated and expanded the achievements made in addressing the financial crisis and maintained the favorable momentum of growth. The industrial reform advanced steadily. The investment channels for insurance funds in fields such as equity investment and real estate investment widened further. Several banks successfully took stakes in insurance companies and the insurance salesmen system reform officially kicked off. Forty-six insurance companies increased RMB 33.17 billion of capital, and eight companies issued RMB 22.55 billion of subordinated debts. The industry posted visibly improved solvency. A total premium income of RMB 1.45 trillion was realized nationwide (+30.4% YoY). The utilization balance of insurance funds reached RMB 4.6 trillion. The funds utilization earnings stood at RMB 201.46 billion and the average ROI was 4.84%.

Column 1

China's 12th Five-year Plan Released

The fourth session of the 11th NPC approved *the Outline of the 12th Five-year Plan on National Economic and Social Development* on March 14, 2011. The 60000-word *Outline* covers 16 chapters, highlighting scientific development and the acceleration of the shift in economic growth mode, and putting forward the guiding ideology, general ideas, objectives and tasks and major measures for the economic and social development in the coming five years. It serves as a grand blueprint for China's economic and social development, a common program of action for the Chinese people of all ethnic groups and an important basis for the government to fulfill its responsibilities in economic regulation, market supervision, social management and public service.

Column 2

The Central Government Launched a Policy Package to Regulate Housing and Commodity Prices

Affected by multiple factors both at home and abroad, the prices of daily necessities, dominated by agricultural products and commodity houses, surged during the second half of 2010, thus giving rise to growing inflationary pressure and bringing uncertainty into the operation of the national economy. Based on scientific judgment of the situations, the Central Committee of the CPC and the State Council employed a wide range of regulatory means and rolled out a package of policies, comprehensively strengthening price regulation and supervision, correctly guiding market expectations, effectively curbing overly heated prices and safeguarding the basic livelihoods of the people.

03

Insurance Industry Serves the Construction of an Economic Society

- Serving and Supporting the Work related to Agriculture, Farmers and Rural Areas
- Promoting Economic Transformation and Upgrading
- Improving the Multi-level Social Security System
- Participating in Social Risk Management

By thoroughly implementing the scientific outlook on development and adhering to the guideline of "doing its own job well and serving overall situations", the insurance industry played a positive role in safeguarding the general development of both the economy and society in 2010.

Insurance Industry Serves the Construction of an Economic Society

Serving and Supporting the Work related to Agriculture, Farmers and Rural Areas

In 2010, the coverage area of China's agricultural insurance continued to expand, with the varieties covered extending from five major grain crops like paddy rice and wheat to cash crops such as timber and rapeseed, the scope of security ranging from planting and stock-raising to farm houses and agricultural machinery, and the areas from the six provinces and autonomous regions for pilot projects to all the provinces, autonomous regions and municipalities directly under the State Council. The number of varieties subsidized by the central finance ministry increased to a total of 14 crops. Local governments nationwide also devised policies successively to support the development of agricultural insurance and launched pilot insurance projects related to edible mushrooms, aquaculture, timber and fruits, and natural rubber, which effectively promoted the development of local agriculture with distinctive features. In 2010, China's agricultural insurance registered a premium income of RMB 13.59 billion, offered risk protection of RMB 394.31 billion and covered 140 million rural households. 680 million mu of major grain, oil and cotton crops were covered, representing 35% of the sown area nationwide; 480 million mu of forests were covered, up 68% YoY; 630 million heads of livestock were covered, including 24.68 million reproductive sows. The full-year's accumulated compensation pay-outs of agricultural insurance reached RMB 9.6 billion, benefiting 19.792 million rural families.

Promoting Economic Transformation and Upgrading

Effort was made to support innovative industrial development. Independent innovation was vigorously advanced, and the pilot projects of such insurance types as scientific and technological insurance, cultural industry insurance and environmental pollution liability insurance were explored in depth with the aim of offering risk protection for innovation-oriented enterprises and of aiming for the low-carbon development of economy. Seven key industries, including electromechanical products, high-tech products, textile products, light industrial products, agricultural products and pharmaceutical products, registered an 80.5% rise in the insurance value.

Efforts were made to secure and promote both domestic and foreign trade. The value of credit insurance for domestic and foreign trade totaled RMB 2418.18 billion (+165.3% YoY). Specifically, the short-term credit insurance value stood at USD 154.33 billion on a cumulative basis (+71% YoY), hitting a record high and surpassing the goal of USD 120 billion set by the State Council. Export finance insurance programs for large-scale complete sets of equipment numbered 45, with a contract value of USD 11.01 billion; the penetration rate of export credit insurance in China's general export rose to 22.8% from 18.6% in 2009.

Effort was made to boost residential consumption. Consumption credit guarantee insurance was developed vigorously, and the value of consumption credit guarantee insurance for houses, cars and other fields amounted to RMB 269.34 billion.

Improving the Multi-level Social Security System

New breakthroughs were made in the health guarantee entrustment management business. Efforts were made to earnestly implement national medical reform policies and participate in the management of the new rural cooperative medical program, basic medical insurance program for urban employees and residents and medical assistance programs, which played a major role in improving China's medical care system. The "Zhanjiang Pattern", which featured the participation of the insurance industry in the medical system reform, caught nationwide attention. The medical security level improved significantly and the coverage grew more extensive without increased input from the governments and without added burdens for the people. The full-year newly added mandatory management funds totaled RMB 8.97 billion, providing compensation and reimbursement services for 21.869 million recipients. In 2010, a health risk security of RMB 23.9 trillion was provided for 840 million recipients and a compensation value of RMB 26.4 billion was paid.

Pension insurance coverage was gradually broadened. By the end of 2010, a total of 7.292 million recipients were offered commercial pension risk security. Corporate annuity business grew rapidly, providing annuity insurance services for 76.346 million recipients. Pension insurance companies collected an annuity trust fee of RMB 35.74 billion, up 35.6% from the beginning of the year; the assets managed under trust reached RMB 103.91 billion, and assets managed as investment totaled RMB 70.9 billion, up 46.5% and 45.9% respectively from early 2010.

Participating in Social Risk Management

In 2010, the insurance industry provided a liability risk security of RMB 33.1 trillion and made a compensation payment of RMB4.4 billion. Specifically, it paid RMB 2.13 billion, RMB 270 million, RMB 1.1 billion and RMB 620 million in compensation funds for public liability, product liability, employer liability and professional liability. Efforts were made to improve the mechanism of risk management with participation from the insurance industry. The insurance industry joined hands with the Ministry of Public Security to implement the already established floating mechanism with linkage between drunk driving and the compulsory insurance rate for motor vehicles that helped improve the compulsory insurance system. The insurance industry worked out *the Measures on the Management of Social Assistance Funds for Road Traffic Accidents* together with relevant ministries and commissions of the state. The development of liability insurances closely related to public interests, such as travel service liability insurance, environmental pollution insurance, safe production insurance, school's liability insurance and medical liability insurance, was highlighted with the aim to positively solve civil disputes, alleviate social contradictions and maintain social stability. Security was provided to positively cope with major disasters and accidents. The insurance industry actively fulfilled its compensation responsibilities during major disasters and accidents such as the Yushu earthquake in Qinghai province, the Yichun air crash in Heilongjiang province and the high-rise building fire in Shanghai. During such major activities as World Expo 2010 Shanghai and Guangzhou Asian Games, the insurance industry played a positive role in risk guarantee, offering risk protection of over RMB 300 billion and covering nearly five million individuals on a cumulative basis.

Column 3

The Insurance Industry Participated in the Construction of Social Security System through Diverse Modes

In 2010, the insurance industry demonstrated its benefits further, actively collaborating with local governments and participating in medical security programs such as the new rural cooperative medical program, the basic medical insurance program for urban residents and the supplementary insurance program for enterprises, public institutions and social groups, which produced notable results and covered 180 million people. The newly added mandatory management funds totaled RMB 8.97 billion and the premium income was RMB 7.06 billion. The recipients of compensation and reimbursement services totaled 21.868 million, and the compensation and reimbursement value was RMB 10.93 billion. During the construction of the service-oriented social security system, typical examples like "Zhanjiang Pattern", "Luoyang Pattern" and "Jinjiang Pattern" emerged in the insurance industry and received extensive praise of people from all walks of life.

Column 4

The Insurance Industry Positively Coped With Major Disasters and Accidents

Pursuant to the uniform deployment by the Central Committee of the CPC and State Council, the insurance industry actively fulfilled its compensation responsibilities during major disasters and accidents such as the Yushu earthquake in Qinghai Province, the Zhouqu mudslide in Gansu Province, the Yichun air crash in Heilongjiang Province and the high-rise building fire in Shanghai in 2010. This effectively secured life and property safety and the steady operation of both the economy and society, and gained the high recognition of people from all walks of life. By the end of 2010, compensation of RMB 3.894 million, RMB 17.708 million, RMB 24.557 million and RMB 9.041 million, respectively, was paid out for the said four major disasters and accidents.

04

Further Improvement of the Insurance Regulatory System

- Responsibilities of China Insurance Regulatory Commission
- Organizational Structure of the CIRC
- Objectives of Supervision
- Further Maturing of the Insurance Regulatory Concept
- Further Implementation of Regulatory Laws and Regulations
- Actual Improvements of Regulatory Capabilities
- Continuous Innovation in Regulation Approaches
- Remarkable Achievements in Regulation over Market Orders
- Effective Prevention of Industrial Risks

Objectives of Supervision

- Protect the interests of the policyholders
- Promote sustainable, rapid and balanced development of the insurance industry
- Prevent and reduce risks

Further Maturing of the Insurance Regulatory Concept

Further implementing the scientific outlook on development and adhering to scientific, lawful and effective regulation, the insurance regulators worked to improve the industrial capability in scientific development by keeping the shifting growth mode, adjusting the structure and promoting insurance innovation. They continued to improve the insurance regulatory system supported by the three pillars (market behavior, solvency and corporate governance) and the five defense lines for preventing risks. While highlighting the prevention of risks facing insurance institutions, the insurance regulators also explored ways for prudent macro-regulation and increasingly made the regulation more scientific, effective and targeted.

Further Implementation of Regulatory Laws and Regulations

Efforts were made to improve corporate governance and internal control regulation systems, to raise the access threshold for shareholders and to regulate corporate equity transfer. The access criteria for senior executives became tougher; rotation training systems for senior executives were established; management and training for senior executives was intensified. Regulation for insurance businesses was strengthened, insurance clause and rate management systems in property insurance companies were improved, dynamic monitoring systems for personal insurance products were established, and reinsurance businesses were regulated. Information disclosure systems were established and improved, and operation transparency was enhanced. A total of 11 departmental rules and a series of regulatory documents including *the Administrative Measures on Equity Interests of Insurance Companies* and *the Administrative Measures on Insurance Group Corporations* were formulated or revised, while current regulatory rules were categorized in a comprehensive way.

Actual Improvements of Regulatory Capabilities

Regulatory institutions were deployed in a scientific manner, with an insurance regulatory bureau set up in Tibet and branches established in all the provinces, autonomous regions and municipalities directly under the State Council. Regulatory coverage was improved. New advancements were made in the extension of regulatory institutions as five regulatory branches in Suzhou, Yantai, Wenzhou, Tangshan and Shantou, respectively, were officially launched. The organizational setup inside the CIRC was improved, with the Department of Solvency Regulation being established to strengthen specialized regulation responsibilities. Thanks to measures for adjusting the leadership group in regulatory branches, intensifying training sessions for regulatory cadres and strengthening the patrol over the branches, the scientific, lawful and effective regulation abilities of regulatory cadres were enhanced further.

Continuous Innovation in Regulation Approaches

Efforts were made to further advance classified regulation, to establish classified regulation mechanisms for branches and to initially form a relatively complete classified regulation system covering legal entities and branches. The insurance industry was instructed to set up a sharing mechanism for vehicle insurance information and a self-inquiry mechanism for policy underwriting and claims information to strengthen the protection of the insured's interests. The First International Joint Conference on Insurance Regulation and the Seventh Sino-US Insurance Dialogue were held, while cooperation with the regulatory institutions of foreign-funded insurance companies in their parent countries was increased. Regulation information development was promoted by devising guidelines and industrial standards and developing the management system for information related to solvency regulation and complaints via letters and visits to further make way for the role of information systems in supporting and guiding industrial development.

Remarkable Achievements in Regulation over Market Orders

Greater efforts were made in on-site inspection centering on the protection of the insured's interests. Inspections to detect false data, non-standard compensation, incompliant reserve withdrawal and sales misguidance, bank post service agency, accident insurance and intermediary businesses was highlighted. The case accountability system was implemented; the responsibilities of 175 people were traced and those suspected of being guilty were handed over to the appropriate judicial authorities. In 2010, the insurance regulatory institutions deployed 1949 inspection groups in total, punished 905 insurance institutions of various types, ordered the replacement of 96 senior executives and investigated 14 commercial bribery cases, which powerfully maintained the market orders.

Effective Prevention of Industrial Risks

Restrictions regarding the regulation of solvency were intensified further, and some insurance companies were urged to improve their solvency through pressure tests, solvency forecasting, regulation prompting and other measures. By the end of 2010, six insurance companies failed to meet the solvency criteria, two fewer than at the end of 2009, and the key indicators of the unqualified companies improved considerably. *The Interim Measures for the Administration of Utilization of Insurance Funds* and a package of supporting policies were launched to strengthen the regulation of insurance funds utilization. The full-process risk prevention and control system was established and improved, while comprehensive risk management was popularized in insurance companies. The financial and business conditions of the overseas shareholders of foreign-funded companies underwent comprehensive investigation to earnestly guard against cross-border transmission of global financial risks.

Column 5

China Held the First International Joint Conference on Insurance Regulation

On December 6, 2010, the CIRC launched the First International Joint Conference on Insurance Regulation in Beijing. This brought together insurance regulators from 11 countries and regions including France, Germany and the US. During the conference, the representatives introduced the measures devised by respective regulatory institutions to meet the global financial crisis as well as the operation of the parent companies that have business branches in China. They also exchanged views on issues such as how to increase communication among the regulatory institutions of multinational insurance groups in parent countries and joint prevention of cross-border risks.

05

Insurance Market Operation

- Business of Non-life Insurance Companies
- Business of Life Insurance Companies
- Professional Reinsurance Business
- Insurance Intermediary Market
- Foreign-funded Insurance Business
- Insurance Assets Management

In 2010, China's insurance industry achieved a total premium income of RMB 1452.8 billion (+30.4% YoY). The insurance penetration was 3.65% ① (+0.33 percentage point YoY) and the insurance density was RMB 1083.4 (+RMB 249 YoY). The indemnity and compensation amounted to RMB 320.04 billion (+2.4% YoY). The total assets of insurance companies reached RMB 5046.72 billion. There were 125 insurance companies (+5 YoY) under eight insurance groups and nine insurance asset management companies.

After implementation of *the No.2 Interpretations for Enterprise Accounting Standards*, the insurance industry reported a total premium income of RMB 1344.27 billion. Specifically, non-life insurance companies realized a premium income of RMB 405.83 billion, life insurance companies a premium income of RMB 894.73 billion, and reinsurance companies a premium income of RMB 43.53 billion.

Insurance Market Operation

Business of Non-life Insurance Companies

Promoted Fast Growth of Premium Income

Boosted by China's macro-economic policies, the non-life insurance businesses continued the strong momentum of growth in 2010, achieving a premium of RMB 402.69 billion (+34.6% YoY); the growth rate increased by 12.2 percentage points higher YoY, the highest level in five years.

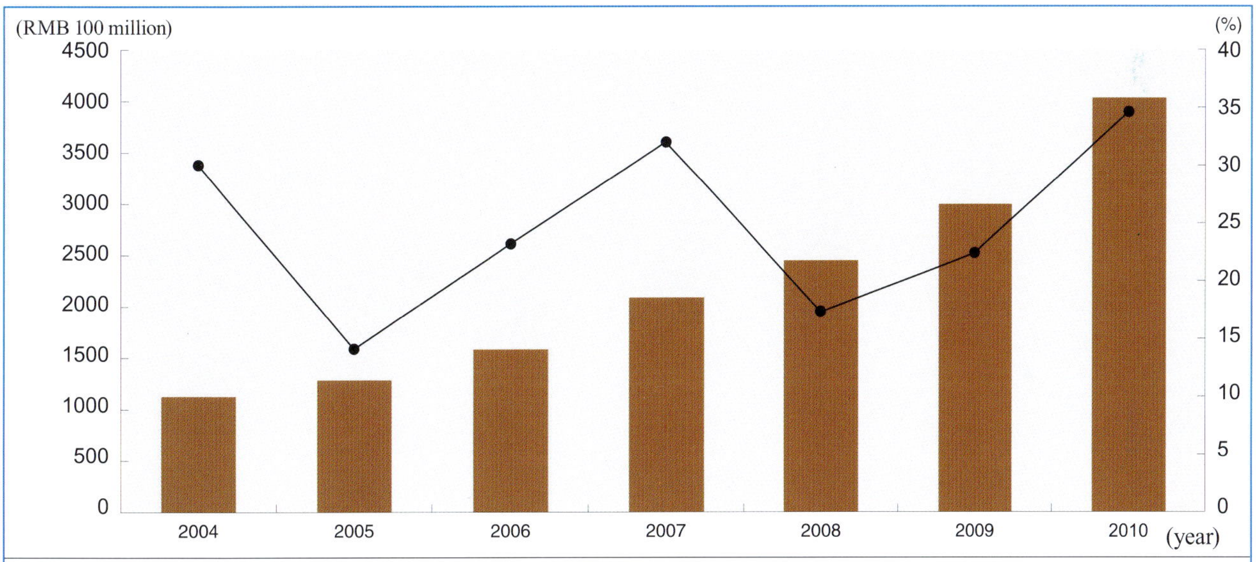

	2004	2005	2006	2007	2008	2009	2010
Premium (left scale)	1124.8	1283.5	1581.1	2086.6	2446.2	2992.9	4026.9
Growth rate (right scale)	30.0	14.1	23.2	32.0	17.3	22.4	34.6

Figure 2 Premium Income and Growth Rate of Non-life Insurance Companies during 2004–2010

The top 5 contributors of premium income consisted of vehicle insurance (RMB 300.42 billion), corporate property insurance (RMB 27.16 billion), agricultural insurance (RMB 13.59 billion), liability insurance (RMB 11.59 billion),and credit insurance(RMB 9.6 billion), which accounted for 90.0% of the total premium income of the property and casualty insurance market.

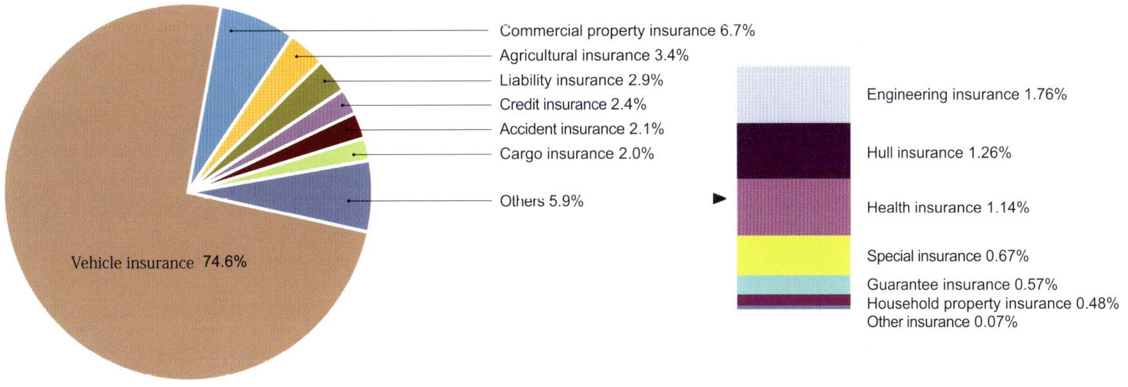

Figure 3 Premium Structure of Non-life Insurance Business in 2010

① Insurance penetration and insurance density were calculated in accordance with the premium data based on the business statistical approach.

Most of the non-life insurance product lines saw continued fast growth, including vehicle insurance (+39.4% YoY), commercial property insurance (+22.7% YoY), liability insurance (+25.7% YoY), credit insurance (+36.6% YoY), cargo insurance (+28.5% YoY), engineering insurance (+37.4% YoY) and marine hull insurance (+21.5% YoY).

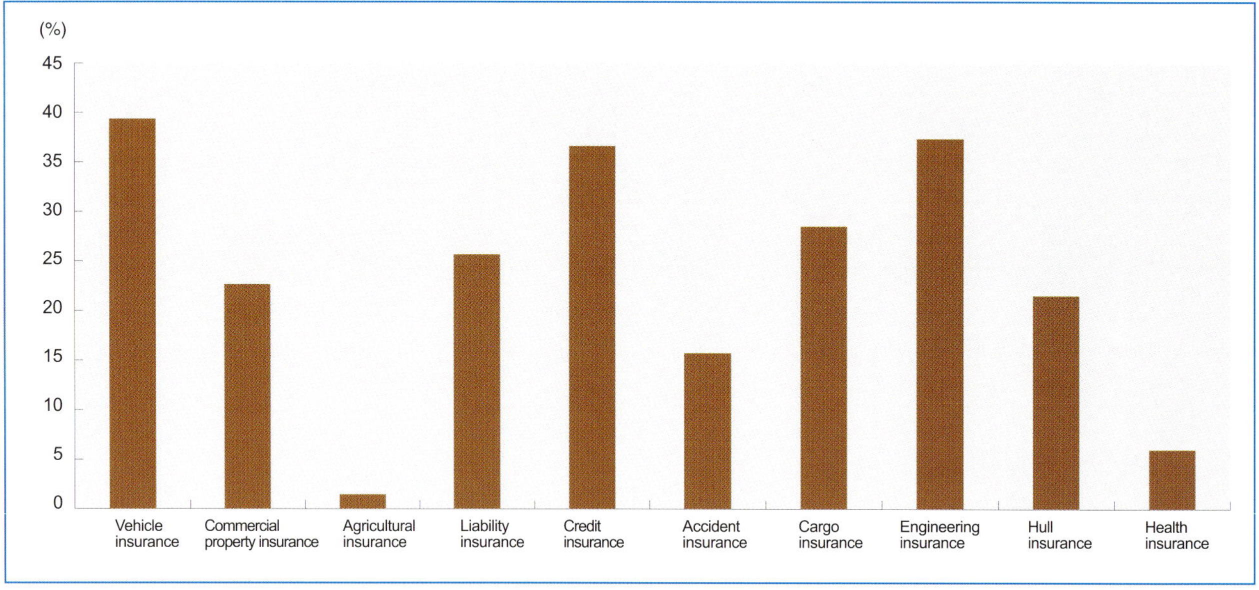

Figure 4 Premium Growth of Major Insurance Product Lines of Non-life Insurance Companies in 2010

Table 1 Top 10 Non-life Insurance Companies by Premium Income in 2010

Rank	Name	Capital structure	Premium income (RMB100 million)	Market share (%)
1	PICC Property and Casualty Company Limited	Domestic	1539.3	38.2
2	Ping An Insurance (Group) Company of China, Ltd.	Domestic	621.2	15.4
3	China Pacific Property Insurance (Group) Co., Ltd.	Domestic	515.3	12.8
4	China United Insurance Holding Company Limited	Domestic	193.4	4.8
5	China Continent Property & Casualty Insurance Company Ltd.	Domestic	138.2	3.4
6	China Life Property and Casualty Insurance Company Limited	Domestic	112.7	2.8
7	Sunshine Property and Casualty Insurance Co., Ltd.	Domestic	106.4	2.6
8	China Export & Credit Insurance Corporation	Domestic	89.1	2.2
9	Tian An Insurance Co., Ltd.	Domestic	80.3	2.0
10	Anbang Property & Casualty Insurance Co., Ltd.	Domestic	70.3	1.8
	Total		3466.2	86.0

Market Players Increased Steadily and the Market Concentration Slightly Recovered

By the end of 2010, China had 56 non-life insurance companies, including 35 domestic-funded companies, one more than last year (Taishan Property Insurance), and 21 foreign-funded companies, two more than the number of the previous year (XL Insurance and Lloyd's Insurance[①]).

The non-life insurance market concentration showed a slight recovery and the top five insurance companies by premium income accounted for 74.6% (+0.5 percentage points YoY) of the market share.

Compensation Pay-outs Continued to Rise

In 2010, non-life insurance companies effected total compensation pay-outs of RMB 181.52 billion (+10.8% YoY) and the growth rate was 0.2 percentage point lower than that of the previous year. Specifically, the compensation for vehicle insurance stood at RMB 137.58 billion (+14.6% YoY), commercial property insurance RMB 11.72 billion (−8.1% YoY), liability insurance RMB 4.4 billion (+13% YoY), cargo

① Approved by the CIRC, Lloyd's Reinsurance (China) Co., Ltd. expanded direct insurance business in 2010. The company changed its nature from reinsurance to property insurance and was renamed Lloyd's Insurance (China) Co., Ltd..

insurance RMB 2.89 billion (+10.4% YoY) and agricultural insurance RMB 9.6 billion (+0.8% YoY). In 2010, the overall expense ratio of earned premium income of non-life insurance companies reached 34.2%, four percentage points lower than that of the year earlier.

Underwriting Profit Remarkably Improved

In 2010, non-life insurance companies registered an underwriting profit of RMB 8.04 billion, and the underwriting profit margin was 2.56%.

Reserve Balance Continued to Grow

By the end of 2010, the unearned premium reserves and outstanding loss reserves of non-life insurance companies reached RMB 328.39 billion (+35.1% YoY), including unearned premium reserves of RMB 176.01 billion and outstanding loss reserves of RMB 152.38 billion.

In 2010, non-life insurance companies withdrew unearned premium reserves of RMB 41.47 billion and outstanding loss reserves of RMB 39.38 billion.

In 2010, non-life insurance companies withdrew undue liability reserves of RMB 41.47 billion and outstanding loss reserves of RMB 39.38 billion.

Column 6

The Insurance Industry Did a Good Job in Offering Insurance Services for World Expo 2010 Shanghai and Guangzhou Asian Games

In 2010, China successively embraced two grand events: World Expo 2010 Shanghai and Guangzhou Asian Games. The insurance industry provided World Expo 2010 Shanghai with installation insurance, property loss insurance, exhibits and fine art insurance services, and provided Guangzhou Asian Games with insurance services related to all the sports events as well as personnel and properties. As the insurance partner of the Expo and Asian Games, PICC P&C developed and underwrote exclusive insurance products for the two mentioned events. It also formulated claim handling service plans and organized special teams for insurance compensation, thus offering powerful support for the successful launch of World Expo 2010 Shanghai and Guangzhou Asian Games.

Column 7

Marketization of the Vehicle Insurance Rate Moved Forward

In June 2010, the CIRC released *the Notice on Carrying out Pilot Projects of the Reform in the Commercial Vehicle Insurance Pricing Mechanism in Shenzhen (BAO JIAN CHAN XIAN [2010] No.619)*, linking vehicle insurance prices with indicators such as violation of traffic rules and compensation records and initiating a reform in the commercial vehicle insurance pricing mechanism, with a view to enhancing the social management function of insurance through rational resources allocation via price leverage.

Column 8

Marine Insurance Embraced New Opportunities for Development

On August 9, 2010, the CIRC approved the pilot establishment of the Marine Insurance Operation Center by PICC P&C and China Pacific Property Insurance Co., Ltd. in Shanghai, with the aim of vigorously promoting the development of marine insurance and further serving the construction of Shanghai's "Two Centers". As a service platform connecting the shipping industry and financial industry, marine insurance faces unprecedented opportunities for development.

Business of Life Insurance Companies[1]

Premium Income Exceeded RMB 1 trillion

In 2010, the premium income of life insurance companies exceeded RMB 1 trillion for the first time and came to RMB 1050.09 billion (+28.9% YoY); the growth rate was nearly 18 percentage points higher than the previous year. The premium income of life insurance companies accounted for 72.3% of gross national premium income. By the end of 2010, the first year premium income of life insurance policies reached RMB 688.25 billion (+26.8% YoY), representing 65.5% of the total premium income of life insurance companies. The installment premium of new policies totaled RMB 180.45 billion (+32.2% YoY), representing 26.2% of the premium of new policies of life insurance companies. The life insurance industry achieved a total profit of RMB 73.63 billion. The overall industrial solvency was sufficient, and the solvency margin was RMB 145.3 billion. Various risks were also prevented.

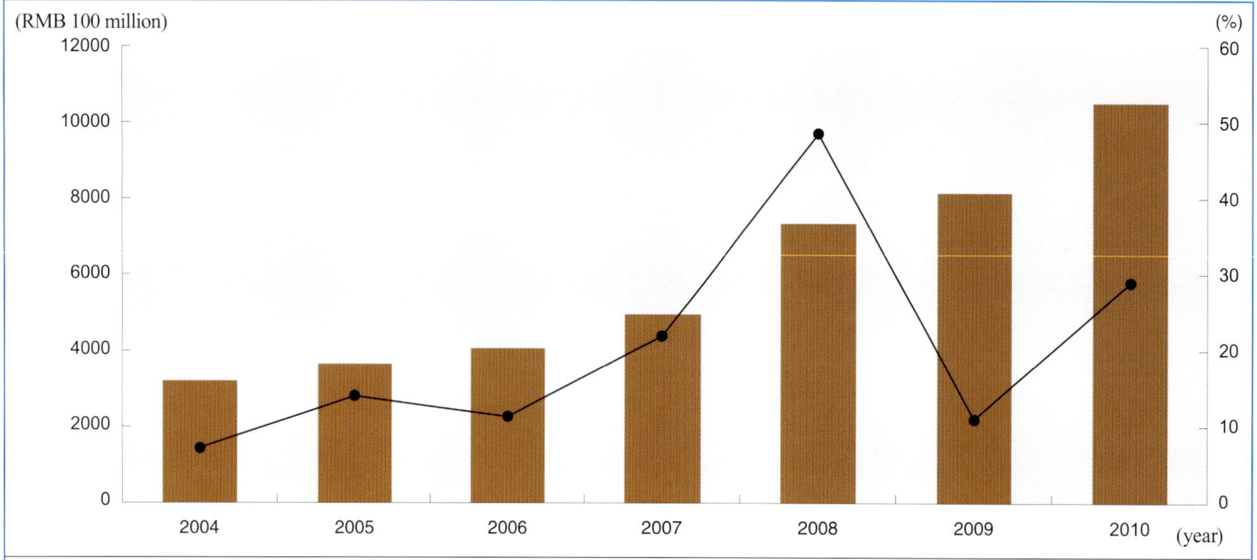

		2004	2005	2006	2007	2008	2009	2010
Premium	(left scale)	3198.2	3644.9	4059.1	4946.5	7342.6	8144.2	10500.9
Growth rate	(right scale)	7.2	14.0	11.3	21.9	48.5	11.0	28.9

Figure 5 Premium Income and Growth Rate of Life Insurance Companies during 2004–2010

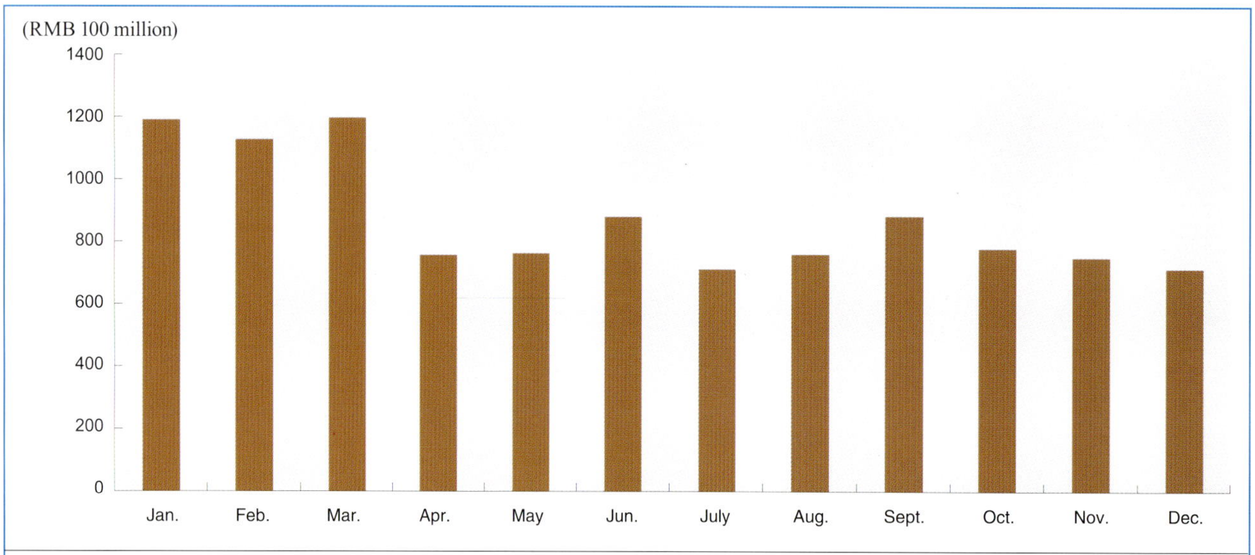

	Jan.	Feb.	Mar.	Apr.	May	Jun.	July	Aug.	Sept.	Oct.	Nov.	Dec.
Premium	1189.6	1127.0	1196.6	756.2	761.9	879.8	711.1	758.6	881.8	777.5	748.2	712.6

Figure 6 Monthly Premium Income of Life Insurance Companies in 2010

Continued Growing Proportion of Participating Life Insurance

In 2010, the life insurance companies further adjusted product structures and strengthened marketing of risk protection products. Participating life insurance took up an increasing proportion in the total life insurance premium income, generating a premium income of RMB 745.48

① Including professional health insurance companies and pension insurance companies.

billion (+40.9% YoY) which represented 71% of the total premium income of life insurance companies (+ six percentage points YoY).
The premium income of universal insurance business was RMB 112.36 billion (+6.5% YoY), accounting for 10.7% of the total premium income of life insurance companies (−2.3 percentage points YoY). The premium income of investment-linked insurance reached RMB 15.28 billion (+3.3% YoY) and made up 1.5% of the total (−0.4 percentage point YoY). The premium income of traditional life insurance totaled RMB 94.82 billion (−1.4% YoY) and represented 9% of the total (−2.8 percentage points YoY).
The combined premium income of health insurance and accident insurance amounted to RMB 82.16 billion (+19.6% YoY) and comprised 7.8% of the total (−0.6 percentage point YoY).

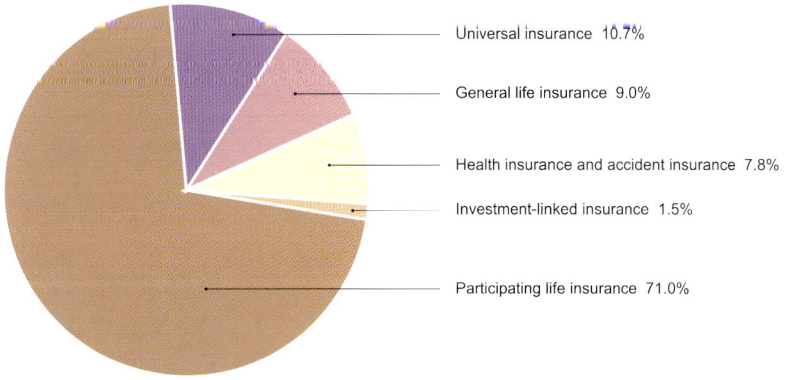

Figure 7　Premium Structure of Life Insurance Business in 2010

Steady Development of Various Channels

Individual agent channel realized a premium income of RMB 431.49 billion (+20.9% YoY), accounting for 41.1% of the total life insurance premium income (−2.7 percentage points YoY).
Bank and post office channel realized a premium income of RMB 524.54 billion (+35% YoY), accounting for 50% of the total life insurance premium income (+2.2 percentage points YoY).
Corporate direct sales channel realized a premium income of RMB 74.95 billion (+39.1% YoY), accounting for 7.1% of the total life insurance premium income (+0.5 percentage point YoY).
Specialist agent channel realized a premium income of RMB 6.27 billion (+6% YoY).
Insurance brokerage channel realized a premium income of RMB 2.67 billion (+65.6% YoY).

Further Optimization of the Market System

By the end of 2010, there were 61 personal insurance companies in China, two more than in the previous year. Specifically, domestic-funded companies numbered 35 (newly increased companies included Zhongrong Life Insurance and Anbang Life Insurance), and foreign-funded companies numbered 26, two fewer than the previous year①. The top five companies by premium income reported a combined market share of 72.8%, down by 4.3 percentage points from a year earlier.

Table 2　Top 10 Life Insurance Companies by Premium Income in 2010

Rank	Name	Capital structure	Premium income (RMB100 million)	Market share (%)
1	China Life Insurance Company, Ltd.	Domestic	3330.4	31.7
2	Ping An Life Insurance Company Of China, Ltd	Domestic	1590.6	15.2
3	New China Life Insurance Co., Ltd.	Domestic	936.4	8.9
4	China Pacific Life Insurance Co., Ltd.	Domestic	920.0	8.8
5	Tai Kang Life Insurance Co., Ltd.	Domestic	867.6	8.3
6	PICC Life Insurance Company Limited	Domestic	824.3	7.9
7	Tai Ping Life Insurance Co., Ltd.	Domestic	330.2	3.1
8	Sino Life Insurance Co., Ltd.	Domestic	153.2	1.5
9	Sunshine Life Insurance Co., Ltd.	Domestic	151.7	1.4
10	PICC Health Insurance Company Limited	Domestic	92.9	0.9
	Total		9197.3	87.7

① In 2010, John Hancock Tianan Life Insurance Co., Ltd. and Sun Life Everbright Life Insurance Co., Ltd. experienced equity changes and changed from joint-venture life insurance companies to domestic-funded life insurance companies. Meanwhile, John Hancock Tianan Insurance Co., Ltd. renamed as Tianan Life Insurance Co., Ltd..

Continued Decline in the Surrender Ratio[1]

In 2010, life insurance companies surrendered an insurance premium of RMB 115.87 billion (+8.3% YoY), and the surrender ratio was 3.05% (−0.48 percentage point YoY). Specifically, domestic-funded life insurance companies posted a surrender ratio of 2.96% to foreign-funded companies' 4.81%.

YoY Decline in Compensation Disbursement

Life insurance companies recorded RMB 138.49 billion (−6.9% YoY) of disbursement of various types of compensation and payment.

Table 3 Life Insurance Companies' Disbursement of Compensation and Payment in 2010

Type	Compensation and payment (RMB 100 million)	Growth rate YOY (%)	Percentage share (%)
Life insurance	1108.7	-12.6	80.1
Health insurance	232.9	27.4	16.8
Accident insurance	43.3	21.3	3.1
Total	1384.9	-6.9	100.0

Professional Reinsurance Business

By the end of 2010, there was one reinsurance (group) company: China Reinsurance (Group) Corporation, and eight professional reinsurance companies, including China Property & Casualty Reinsurance Company Ltd., China Life Reinsurance Company Ltd., Munich Re Beijing Branch, Swiss Re Beijing Branch, General Reinsurance AG, Shanghai Branch, Scor China, Hannover Re Shanghai Branch and Taiping Reinsurance Beijing Branch.

In 2010, the total reinsurance premium income of China's reinsurance companies reached RMB 43.55 billion (+0.5% YoY). The total reinsurance compensation disbursement of nationwide reinsurance companies totaled RMB 17.25 billion (−27% YoY).

Insurance Intermediary Market

In 2010, the premium income achieved through various insurance intermediary channels reached RMB 1094.13 billion[2] (+19.4% YoY), accounting for 75.4% of the national total.

Table 4 Premium Income and Percentage of Various Insurance Intermediary Channels in 2010

Sales channel	Insurance agencies	Insurance brokers	Cross-sector intermediaries	Insurance sales representatives	Total
Premium income (RMB 100 million)	481.7	313.1	5464.4	4682.1	10941.3
Growth rate YoY (%)	46.5	28.0	22.5	13.5	19.4
Percentage (%)	3.3	2.1	37.7	32.3	75.4

Professional Insurance Intermediaries

In 2010, there were 2550 (−20% YoY) professional insurance intermediaries in China, including 1853 insurance agencies, 392 insurance brokers and 305 surveyors and loss adjusters.

In 2010, the operating income of nationwide professional insurance intermediaries totaled RMB 11.84 billion (+32.7% YoY), and the net profit RMB 820 million (+71.9% YoY). Specifically, professional insurance agencies achieved an agent fee income of RMB 6.31 billion (+40.8% YoY) and a net profit of RMB 200 million (+134.1% YoY). Insurance brokers achieved an operating income of RMB 4.4 billion (+32.8% YoY) and a net profit of RMB 570 million (+62.2% YoY). Surveyors and loss adjusters achieved an operating income of RMB 1.16

① The surrender premium and surrender ratio were data based on the business statistical approach.

② Part of the data came from the statements submitted to relevant insurance regulatory authorities by insurance companies and professional insurance intermediary agencies.

billion (+2.7% YoY) and a net profit of RMB 50 million (+18.4% YoY).

Cross-sector Insurance Intermediaries

By the end of 2010, there were 189877 (+27.5% YoY) cross-sector insurance intermediaries nationwide and the agent fees income totaled RMB 28.35 billion (+27.6% YoY).

Table 5 Business Structure of Cross-sector Insurance Intermediaries in 2010

Channel	Number of Agencies	Share (%)	Premium income (RMB 100 million)	Share(%)	Fees Income (RMB 100 million)	Share (%)
Bank	113632	59.9	3503.8	64.1	149.9	52.9
Post	24845	13.1	896.0	16.4	34.3	12.1
Railway	435	0.2	3.1	0.1	0.4	0.1
Aviation	2171	1.1	7.2	0.1	4.3	1.5
Vehicle	23859	12.6	424.8	7.8	51.8	18.3
Others	24935	13.1	629.6	11.5	42.8	15.1
Total	189877	100.0	5464.5	100.0	283.5	100.0

Insurance Sales Representatives

By the end of 2010, there were 3.298 million (+13.5% YoY) insurance sales representatives, including 2.879 million (+11.7% YoY) life insurance sales representatives and 419000 (+27.4% YoY) property insurance sales representatives.

Foreign-funded Insurance Business

In 2010, the premium income of foreign-funded insurance companies reached RMB 63.43 billion (+38.5% YoY), and the growth rate was 21 percentage points higher compared with the previous year; the premium income accounted for 4.4% (+0.3 percentage point YoY) of the national total. The disbursement of various types of compensation and payments totaled RMB 7.37 billion (+24.5% YoY).

Column 9

Bancassurance Business Regulated

Since the latter half of 2010, the CBRC and CIRC have successively released *the Notice on Further Strengthening the Compliance Sales and Risk Management Related to Insurance Agency Business by Commercial Banks (YIN JIAN FA [2010] No.90), the Guidelines on Regulating the Insurance Agency Business by Commercial Banks (BAO JIAN FA [2011] No.10)* and other regulatory documents, carrying out all-round and systematic regulation over the bancassurance market by multiple means like intensifying the control of over-sales behaviors and regulating the management of bancassurance products and agency fees. The move centered on the protection of consumers' rights and interests, and targeted the key parts and major risks in the operation of bancassurance.

Column 10

Inspection of Insurance Companies' Intermediary Businesses Carried out

In 2010, the CIRC conducted a nationwide inspection of the intermediary businesses engaged by insurance companies, and focused on prominent problems such as insurance companies' acts of deception, inflated costs and illegal obtaining of funds. A total of 44 inspection groups were discharged to conduct inspections of 58 grass-roots institutions under 21 insurance legal entities. A figure totaling RMB 140 million of funds illegally obtained by insurance companies was uncovered; 117 insurance companies and insurance intermediary institutions were punished by law. The insurance business license of one provincial-level corporate business department was revoked; fines were imposed on RMB 13.23 million of funds. A total of 138 persons in charge were investigated and two persons were forbidden from any involvement in the insurance industry for the rest of their lives. Fifteen illegal and criminal clues were transferred to judicial authorities. As a result of the inspection, orders in the intermediary market were further regulated, potential risks were controlled, and the interests of the insured were afforded serious protection.

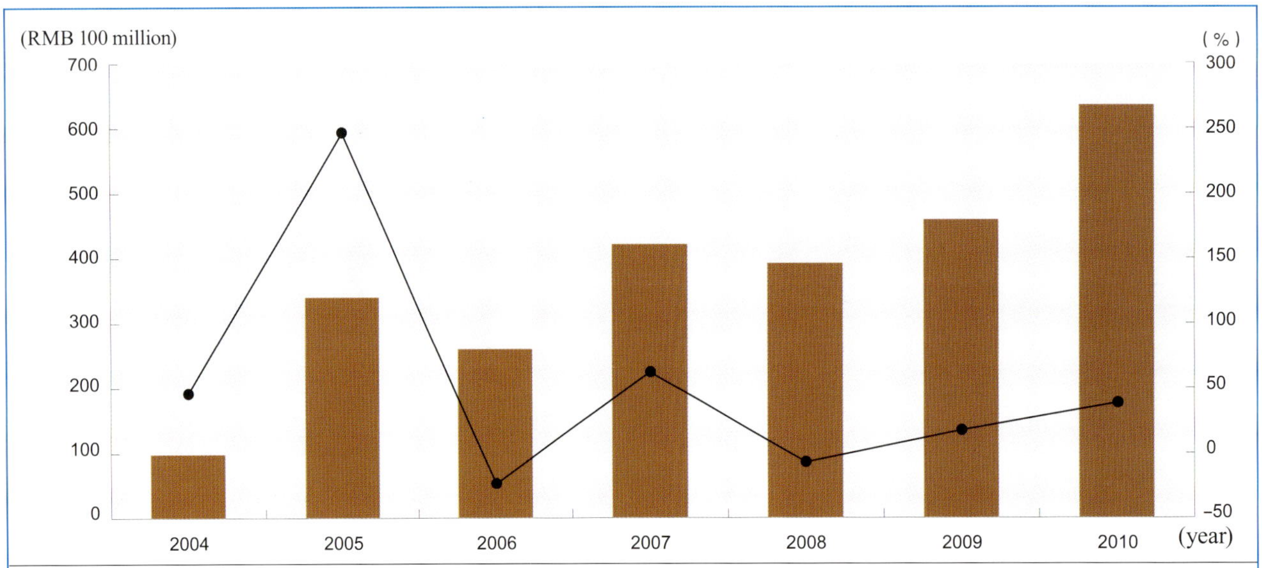

	2004	2005	2006	2007	2008	2009	2010
Premium (left scale)	97.9	339.3	259.4	420.5	391.2	458.0	634.3
Growth rate (right scale)	45.7	246.3	−23.5	62.1	−7.0	17.5	38.5

Figure 8 Premium Income and Growth Rate of Foreign-funded Insurance Companies during 2004–2010

In 2010, the premium income of non-life insurance companies acheived a figure of RMB 4.28 billion (+34.9% YoY), accounting for 1.1% of the total premium income of non-life insurance companies nationwide. The premium income from cargo insurance, commercial property insurance and liability insurance made up 73.2% of the foreign non-life insurance business. The compensation disbursement of foreign-funded non-life insurance companies reached RMB 1.6 billion (+38.2% YoY), and the general expense ratio of the earned premium was 60.3%.

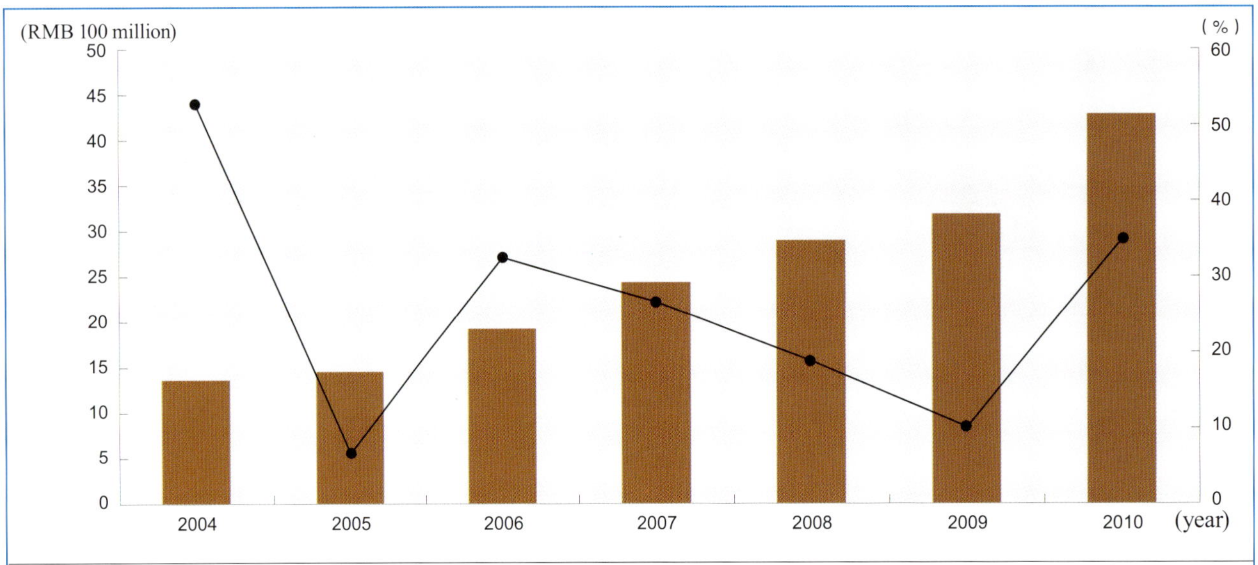

	2004	2005	2006	2007	2008	2009	2010
Premium (left scale)	13.6	14.5	19.2	24.3	28.9	31.8	42.8
Growth rate (right scale)	52.8	6.7	32.5	26.6	18.8	10.1	34.9

Figure 9 Premium Income and Growth Rate of Foreign-funded Non-life Insurance Companies during 2004–2010

Column 11

Ice-breaking in the Reform of the Insurance Salesmen System

On October 21, 2010, the CIRC released *the Opinion on Reforming and Improving the Management System for Insurance Salesmen,* specifying the guideline of "stabilizing teams, enhancing quality and innovating modes", proposing to "build an insurance sales system featuring clear legal relations, specific management responsibilities, equal rights and obligations, linkage between revenue and performance, complete basic security, legal compliance, diverse channels and dynamic vitality", and setting the reform goal of "fostering an insurance marketing team with sound professional behaviors, high professional quality and sustained development potentials". Initiating the reform in the salesmen management system is of far-reaching significance for the sustained and healthy development of the insurance industry, the protection of the systematic risks in the insurance market and safeguarding the interests of the insured.

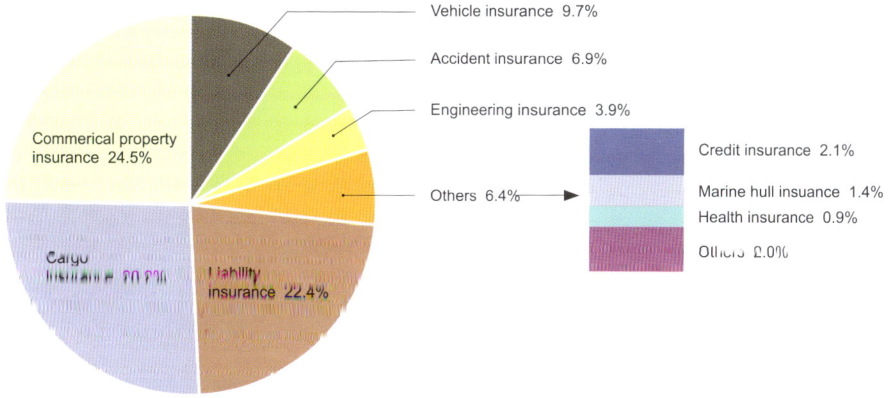

Figure 10 Business Structure of Foreign-funded Non-life Insurance Companies

In 2010, the premium income of foreign-funded life insurance companies achieved a figure of RMB 59.15 billion (+38.8% YoY), accounting for 5.6% of the total premium income of the life insurance companies nationwide. The compensation disbursement of foreign-funded life insurance companies was RMB 5.77 billion (+21.3% YoY), and the surrender rate was 4.81%.

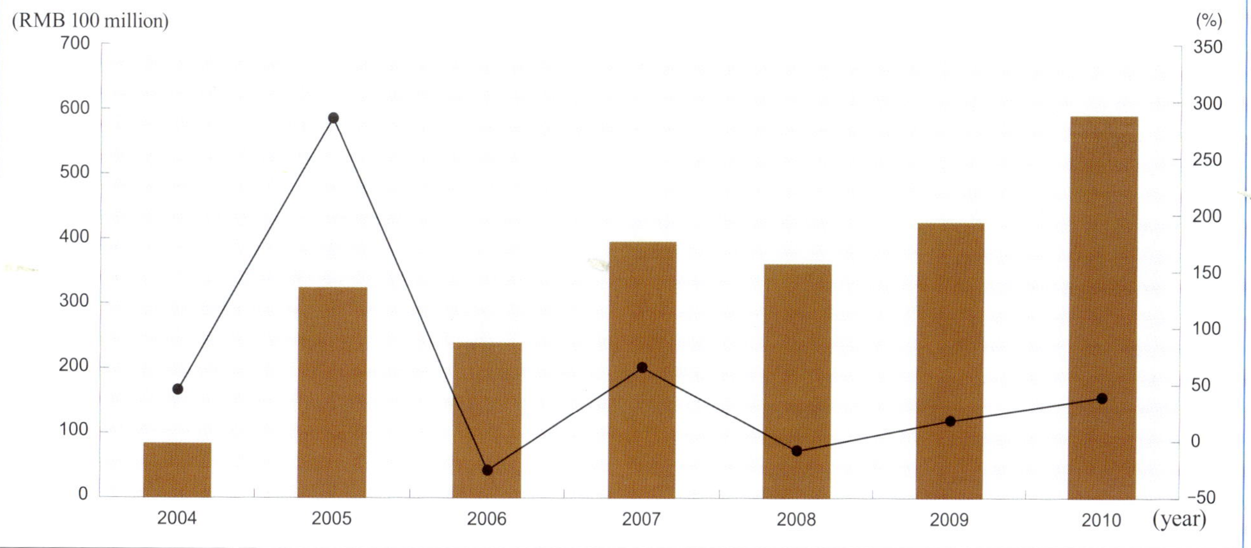

	2004	2005	2006	2007	2008	2009	2010
Premium (left scale)	84.4	324.8	240.2	396.2	362.3	426.3	591.5
Growth rate (right scale)	44.8	284.7	−26.0	64.9	−8.6	18.1	38.8

Figure 11 Premium Income and Growth Rate of Foreign-funded Life Insurance Companies during 2004–2010

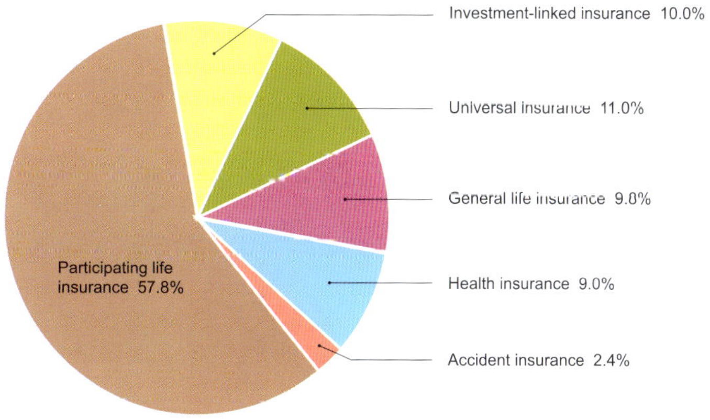

Figure 12 Business Structure of Foreign-funded Life Insurance Companies

The reinsurance premium income of foreign-funded reinsurance companies was RMB 17.68 billion (+43% YoY), accounting for 40.6% of the total reinsurance premium income of nationwide reinsurance companies, and the reinsurance compensation disbursement totaled RMB 4.38 billion (−16.5% YoY).

By the end of 2010, there were 52 foreign-funded insurance companies consisting of 21 non-life insurance companies, 26 life insurance companies and 5 reinsurance companies.

Table 6 Top Five Foreign-funded Non-life Insurance Companies by Market Share[1]

No.	2010 Name	2010 Market Share of Foreign-funded Non-life Insurance Companies (%)	2009 Name	2009 Market Share of Foreign-funded Non-life Insurance Companies (%)
1	CHARTIS	23.8	CHARTIS	25.5
2	Tokio Marine	9.7	Tokio Marine	10.4
3	Mitsui Sumitomo	9.5	Mitsui Sumitomo	10.3
4	Liberty Mutual	8.9	Liberty Mutual	8.3
5	Samsung	8.5	Samsung	8.1
	Total	60.4	Total	62.6

Table 7 Top Five Foreign-funded Life Insurance Companies by Market Share

No.	2010 Name	2010 Market Share of Foreign-funded Non-life Insurance Companies (%)	2009 Name	2009 Market Share of Foreign-funded Non-life Insurance Companies (%)
1	AIA	14.3	AIA	18.9
2	Cenerali	10.4	Cenerali	10.6
3	Huatai Life	10.3	Huatai Life	10.2
4	CITIC-Prudential	9.2	Aviva-COFCO	9.8
5	Aviva-COFCO	8.3	CITIC-Prudential	9.4
	Total	52.5	Total	58.9

In 2010, foreign-funded insurance companies still focused their businesses on the cities that had been opened earlier, such as Shanghai, Beijing, Guangzhou and Shenzhen. The premium income of the foreign-funded insurance companies in the above four cities accounted for 65.3% of foreign premiums of the whole country, up 1.9 percentage points on a year-on-year basis.

Table 8 Development of Foreign-funded Insurance Companies in Shanghai, Beijing, Guangzhou and Shenzhen

City	Foreign-funded Insurance Companies			Foreign-funded Non-life Insurance Companies			Foreign-funded Life Insurance Companies		
	Premium income (RMB 100 million)	Up YoY (%)	Market share (%)	Premium income (RMB 100 million)	Up YoY (%)	Market share (%)	Premium income (RMB 100 million)	Up YoY (%)	Market share (%)
Shanghai	158.6	40.5	25.0	17.5	28.7	40.9	141.1	42.2	23.9
Beijing	157.6	57.2	24.8	7.5	86.6	17.5	150.1	54.9	25.4
Guangzhou	69.5	29.5	11.0	6.4	27.3	15.0	63.1	29.8	10.7
Shenzhen	28.5	23.9	4.5	2.9	25.6	6.8	25.6	23.8	4.3

Insurance Assets Management

The Scale of Insurance Assets Saw Rapid Growth

In 2010, China continued to implement the stimulus package aimed to meet the international financial crisis. This resulted in a further upward trend in the national economy, continued expansion in insurance premium income and a rapid increase in the scale of assets. By the end of 2010, insurance companies boasted total assets of RMB 5046.72 billion. The utilization balance of insurance funds reached a figure of RMB 4604.61 billion (+23.1% YoY).

The Insurance Investment Yielded Steady Returns

The whole insurance industry vigorously seized changes in the capital market, continued to optimize asset allocation and effectively reduced investment risks. In 2010, the return on capital utilization achieved by insurance companies amounted to RMB 201.46 billion, and the average rate of return was 4.84%. Specifically, interest income was RMB 38.6 billion (19.2%), bond investment return RMB 94.3 billion (46.8%), securities investment return RMB 27.13 billion (13.5%), and stock (equity) investment return RMB 35.37 billion (17.6%).

① Calculated based on the premium date of the companies.

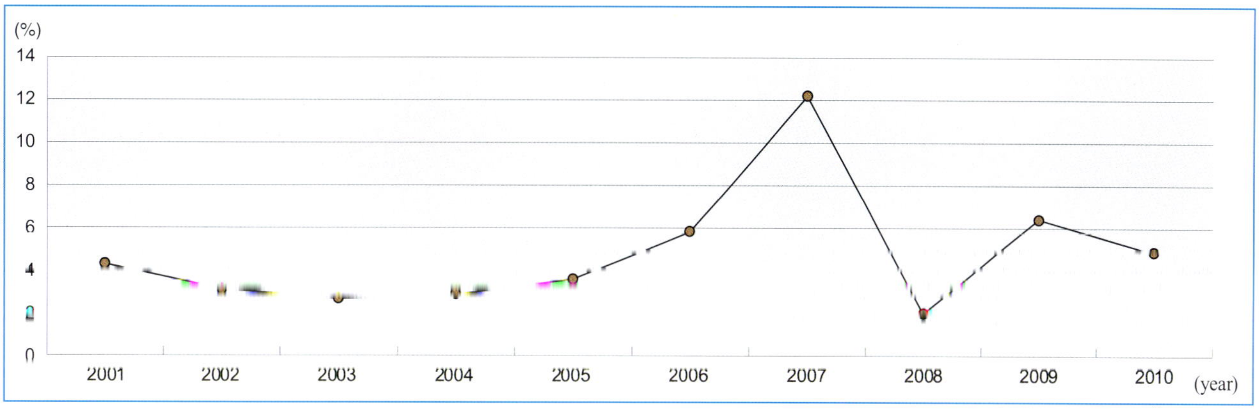

Figure 13 Rate of Return on Investment of the Insurance Companies during 2001–2010

Insurance Investment Channels Further Expanded

In 2010, the CIRC successively released four important rules and regulatory documents, namely *the Interim Measures for the Administration of Utilization of Insurance Funds, Notice on Adjusting the Investment Policies for Insurance Funds, the Interim Measures for Equity Investment with Insurance Funds, the Interim Measures for the Investment of Insurance Funds in Real Estate,* further expanding the channels for the utilization of insurance funds. Currently, insurance investment covers a wide range of fields, including bonds, stocks, funds, equity, infrastructures, real estate and overseas investment, broadening the room for asset allocation by insurance companies while raising the bar for insurance institutions in investment capabilities and risk management and control.

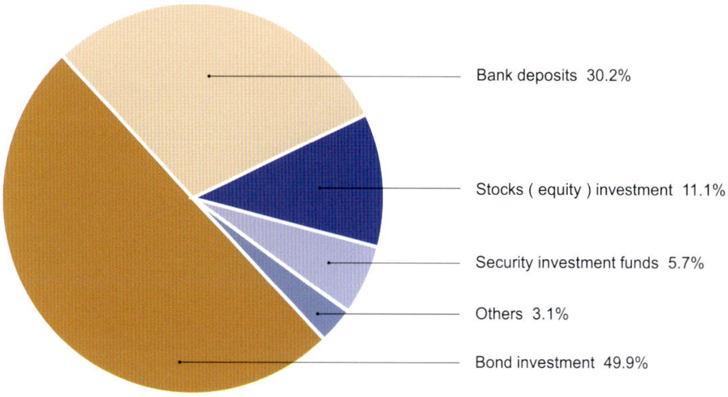

Figure 14 Application Structures of Insurance Funds

Insurance Investment Effectively Served Social Development

The accelerated entry of insurance investment in pension, medical care, auto service and other real estate fields related to insurance businesses helped extend the insurance service industrial chain and make insurance services more specialized and diversified. The presence of insurance companies in equity investment made a number of insurance asset management companies initiate the plans on infrastructure debt investment, which effectively served national economic construction and social development.

06

Development Prospects for China's Insurance Market in 2011

- The Generally Good Economic Environment Offered More Opportunities for the Development of the Insurance Industry
- The Insurance Market is Expected to Maintain Steady Development with the Shift of Growth Mode being the Theme

Development Prospects for China's Insurance Market in 2011

The Generally Good Economic Environment Offered More Opportunities for the Development of the Insurance Industry

2011 is the first year of the 12th Five-year Plan period and a year that marks the deeper progress of economic globalization, accelerated adjustment of world economy, as well as a breakthrough in scientific and technological innovation and industrial transformation. China's industrialization, informatization, urbanization, marketization and internationalization has further advanced, resulting in huge market demand, higher labor quality, increasingly improved infrastructures and a stable social environment. Together, these factors lay a sound foundation for the development of the insurance industry. China will implement positive fiscal policies, shift the moderately loose monetary policies to prudent ones, continue strengthening and improving macro-economic regulation, and speed up the transformation of the economic growth mode and economic restructuring. It will vigorously develop social undertakings, earnestly push forward resource conservation and environmental protection, focus on the improvement of the people's livelihood and deepen the reform and opening-up in an all-round way. Thus, the insurance industry will enjoy broader room for development. Meanwhile, China still faces extremely complex situations and numerous uncertainties as the system contradictions and structural problems overlap each other. This raises the bar for the insurance industry with regard to internal control, restructuring and sound and fast development.

The Insurance Market is Expected to Maintain Steady Development with the Shift of Growth Mode being the Theme

In 2011, the insurance industry will enter into a key period featuring fast growth, prominent contradictions and problems and all-round transformation. The opportunities and challenges coexist, while development goes side by side with risks. The insurance industry will focus more on improving independent innovation capabilities, enhancing employee quality, upgrading operation and management, and accelerating the shift from extensive development to intensive development. It will focus more on fostering new business sources to satisfy the extensive demand for the insurance industry arising from economic and social development and on accelerating the transformation from homogenized competition to differentiated competition. The insurance industry will focus more on its sustained development to offer the public trustworthy and quality insurance services with high added value and on the accelerated shift from extensive resource development to harmonious utilization of resources. Hence, China's insurance market is expected to maintain a momentum of steady and healthy growth as the insurance industry makes a continuous effort to achieve innovative development.

07

Appendix

- Important Regulatory Trends of China's Insurance Market in 2010
- Major Economic and Social Indicators of China during 2003–2010
- Major Financial Indicators of China during 2003–2010
- Major Insurance Indicators of China during 2003–2010
- Major Economic and Financial Websites in China

>> Appendix 1

Important Regulatory Trends of China's Insurance Market in 2010

1. The Guiding Opinions on Pursuing the Liabilities for Cases Involving Insurance Institutions

This was released by the CIRC on January 29, 2010 and took effect as of July 1, 2010. It is aimed at intensifying the efforts in pursuing the liabilities of legal entities and senior executives at various levels, raising the liability awareness of legal entities and executives, pushing insurance companies to actively enhance internal controls and better prevent and control risks related to cases.

2. The Measures for the Administration of Insurance Group Companies (For Trial Implementation)

This was released by the CIRC on March 12, 2010. The Measures define the general framework and basic contents for the supervision of insurance group companies, and specify provisions on the access conditions, corporate governance, capital management, information disclosure and supervision and administration for insurance group companies, which together are conducive for further intensifying supervision of insurance companies and groups, protecting risks facing insurance groups and promoting the healthier development of the insurance industry.

3. The Guiding Opinions on the Financial Support for the Revitalization and Prosperity of Cultural Industries

This was jointly released on March 19, 2010 by nine ministries and commissions: the People's Bank of China, the Publicity Department of the CPC, the Ministry of Finance, the Ministry of Culture, the State Administration of Radio Film and Television of China, the General Administration of Press and Publication, China Banking Regulatory Commission, China Securities Regulatory Commission and CIRC. It is the first macro-financial guiding policy centered on offering financial support to the prosperity of China's cultural industries in recent years and is of great significance for further improving and enhancing the financial services for China's cultural industries and supporting the revitalization and prosperity of the cultural industries.

4. The Administrative Measures for Equities of Insurance Companies

This was released by the CIRC on May 4, 2010 and came into effect as of June 10, 2010. The Measures further regulate equity transfer by insurance companies and strengthen the obligations of shareholders, thus making it of great significance to intensifying the supervision over the equities of insurance companies, maintaining the steady operation of insurance companies and safeguarding the legitimate rights and interests of both investors and insureds.

5. The Administrative Measures for the Information Disclosure of Insurance Companies

Released by the CIRC on May 12, 2010, the Measures came into effect as of June 12, 2010, marking a crucial step by the insurance industry towards ensuring information transparency. They help safeguard the legitimate rights and interests of insurance applicants, insureds and beneficiaries, improve the governance structure of insurance companies, perfect the insurance supervision system, enhance the operational efficiency of the insurance market and maintain the steady and sound development of the insurance industry.

6. The Interim Measures for the Classified Supervision of Branch Offices of Insurance Companies

Released by the CIRC on May 25, 2010, their aim is to improve the efficiency of supervision by insurance regulatory bureaus over branches of insurance companies, to regulate the classified supervision by insurance regulatory bureaus over branches of insurance companies and to further optimize the classified supervision system.

7. The Interim Measures for the Administration of Utilization of Insurance Funds

This was released by the CIRC on July 30, 2010 and became effective as of August 31, 2010. The Measures further specify the principles, forms, decision operation mechanism, risk management and control, and regulation and administration resources related to the utilization of insurance funds. They are of great significance to regulating the utilization of insurance funds and ensuring the safety of the utilization of insurance funds.

8. The Basic Rules for the Internal Control of Insurance Companies

This was released by the CIRC on August 10, 2010 and took effect as of January 1, 2011. They are of great significance for further intensification of the internal control of insurance companies, for improving risk prevention and operational capabilities of insurance companies and for promoting compliance and prudent operation by insurance companies.

9. The Interim Measures for Equity Investment with Insurance Funds, and the Interim Measures for the Investment of Insurance Funds in Real Estate

Released by the CIRC on September 3, 2010, these are intended to regulate the investment in equities and real estate with insurance funds and are of great significance to improving the match between insurance assets and debts, alleviating investment pressure, preventing investment risks and safeguarding asset safety.

10. The Opinions on Reforming and Improving the System for Insurance Salesmen Administration

Released by the CIRC on September 20, 2010, these specify the general ideas and goals for the reform in China's insurance salesmen system and are of far-reaching significance for maintaining the healthy development of the insurance industry, preventing systematic risks in the insurance market and protecting the interests of insureds.

Table 7 Total Volume of Foreign Trade, 2003-2010

Year	Total Volume of Foreign Trade (USD 100 million)	Growth Rate (%)
2003	8512	37.1
2004	11548	35.7
2005	14221	23.2
2006	17607	23.8
2007	21738	23.5
2008	25616	17.8
2009	22072	-13.9
2010	29728	34.7

Source: China Statistical Yearbook and Statistical Communiqué by the National Bureau of Statistics of China in previous years.

Table 8 Total Fiscal Expenditure, 2003-2010

Year	Total Fiscal Revenue (RMB 100 million)	Growth Rate (%)	Total Fiscal Expenditure (RMB 100 million)	Growth Rate (%)
2003	21715.3	14.9	24650.0	11.8
2004	26396.5	21.6	28486.9	15.6
2005	31649.3	19.9	33930.3	19.1
2006	38760.2	22.5	40422.7	19.1
2007	51321.8	32.4	49781.4	23.2
2008	61330.4	19.5	62592.7	25.7
2009	68518.3	11.7	76299.9	21.9
2010	83080.3	21.3	89575.4	17.4

Source: China Statistical Yearbook and Statistical Communiqué by the National Bureau of Statistics of China in previous years.

>>Appendix 3

Major Financial Indicators of China during 2003-2010

Table 1 Deposits Balance of National Urban and Rural Residents, 2003-2010

Year	Deposits Balance of National Urban and Rural Residents (RMB 100 million)	Annual Increase (RMB 100 million)
2003	103617	16632
2004	119555	15929
2005	141051	21497
2006	161587	20544
2007	172534	10947
2008	217885	45351
2009	260772	42887
2010	303302	42530

Source: China Statistical Yearbook and Statistical Communique by the National Bureau of Statistics of China in previous years.

Table 2 Number of Listed Companies, Shares Issued, Capital Raised, 2003-2010

Year	Number of Listed Companies	Amount Issued (100 million shares)	Raised Capital of Shares (RMB 100 million)
2003	1287	281.4	1357.8
2004	1377	227.9	1510.9
2005	1381	567.1	1882.5
2006	1434	1287.8	5594.3
2007	1550	637.2	8680.2
2008	1625	180.3	3852.2
2009	1718	400.1	4967.7
2010	2063	—	—

Source: China Statistical Yearbook and Statistical Communique by the National Bureau of Statistics of China in previous years.

Table 3 Gold Reserve and Foreign Exchange Reserve, 2003-2010

Year	Gold Reserve (10000 ounce)	Foreign Exchange Reserve (USD 100 million)
2003	1929	4032.5
2004	1929	6099.3
2005	1929	8188.7
2006	1929	10663.4
2007	1929	15282.5
2008	1929	19460.3
2009	3389	23991.5
2010	3389	28473.4

Source: China Statistical Yearbook 2010 and Website of the People's Bank of China (www.pbc.gov.cn).

Table 4 Annual Exchange Rate, 2003-2010

Year	RMB/USD (Ending Balance)	RMB/USD (Average)
2003	8.2767	8.2770
2004	8.2765	8.2768
2005	8.0702	8.1949
2006	7.8087	7.9735
2007	7.3046	7.3676
2008	6.8346	6.8424
2009	6.8282	6.8279
2010	6.6227	6.6515

Source: Website of the People's Bank of China (www.pbc.gov.cn).

>>Appendix 4

Major Insurance Indicators of China during 2003–2010

Table 1 Distribution of Premium Income, 2003–2010

Year	Insurance Premium		Life Insurance Companies		Non-life Insurance Companies	
	Absolute Value (RMB 100 million)	Growth Rate (%)	Absolute Value (RMB 100 million)	Growth Rate (%)	Absolute Value (RMB 100 million)	Growth Rate (%)
2003	3848.8	26.3	2983.2	31.1	865.6	12.0
2004	4323.0	12.3	3198.2	7.2	1124.8	30.0
2005	4928.4	14.0	3644.9	14.0	1283.1	14.1
2006	5640.2	14.4	4059.1	11.3	1581.1	23.2
2007	7033.4	25.0	4946.5	21.9	2086.6	32.0
2008	9789.1	39.2	7342.6	48.5	2446.2	17.3
2009	11137.3	13.8	8144.2	11.0	2992.9	22.4
2010	14528.0	30.4	10500.9	28.9	4026.9	34.6

Table 2 Distribution of Premium Income by Region in 2010

Region	Original Insurance Premium Income			Property and Casualty Insurance			Life Insurance		
	Accumulative (RMB 10000)	YoY Growth (%)	Proportion (%)	Accumulative (RMB 10000)	YoY Growth (%)	Proportion (%)	Accumulative (RMB 10000)	YoY Growth (%)	Proportion (%)
National total	145279714.55	30.44	100.00	38956424.70	35.47	100.00	106323289.85	28.70	100.00
1. Independent Business Income of Headquarters	426161.11	66.09	0.29	415787.55	71.59	1.07	10373.56	–63.05	0.01
2. East Region	85075461.50	30.53	58.56	23259641.22	34.14	59.71	61815820.28	29.22	58.14
Beijing	9664550.65	38.54	6.65	2123030.12	29.12	5.45	7541520.53	41.45	7.09
Tianjin	2140074.43	41.46	1.47	651335.45	42.23	1.67	1488738.98	41.12	1.40
Hebei	7464041.36	24.18	5.14	1929059.18	49.92	4.95	5534982.18	17.16	5.21
Liaoning	4538131.73	31.35	3.12	1185761.26	37.13	3.04	3352370.47	29.42	3.15
Dalian	1510482.50	29.84	1.04	435649.33	32.50	1.12	1074833.17	28.80	1.01
Shanghai	8838593.40	32.91	6.08	1892201.38	[illegible]	[illegible]	[illegible]	35.35	6.53
Jiangsu	11626736.02	28.09	8.00	3119064.97	36.57	8.01	8507671.05	25.23	8.00
Zhejiang	6903428.92	28.29	4.75	2594736.65	32.16	6.66	4308692.27	26.07	4.05
Ningbo	1440614.77	34.08	0.99	661979.99	29.60	1.70	778634.78	38.14	0.73
Fujian	3460657.01	27.11	2.38	998918.00	37.46	2.56	2461739.01	23.34	2.32
Xiamen	775466.53	32.80	0.53	282012.95	45.25	0.72	493453.58	26.60	0.46
Shandong	8762161.50	29.32	6.03	2415716.12	39.09	6.20	6346445.38	25.95	5.97
Qingdao	1538525.65	33.43	1.06	495450.84	44.29	1.27	1043074.81	28.82	0.98
Guangdong	12317606.32	28.37	8.48	3090578.26	29.26	7.93	9227028.06	28.07	8.68
Shenzhen	3614914.96	33.10	2.49	1205660.56	24.21	3.09	2409254.40	38.05	2.27
Hainan	479475.77	44.99	0.33	178486.17	50.58	0.46	300989.60	41.87	0.28

continue

Region	Original Insurance Premium Income			Property and Casualty Insurance			Life Insurance		
	Accumulative (RMB 10000)	YoY Growth (%)	Proportion (%)	Accumulative (RMB 10000)	YoY Growth (%)	Proportion (%)	Accumulative (RMB 10000)	YoY Growth (%)	Proportion (%)
3. Middle Region	33714166.80	30.52	23.21	7481692.94	39.14	19.21	26232473.86	28.25	24.67
Shanxi	3652982.88	26.29	2.51	929384.88	38.45	2.39	2723598.00	22.62	2.56
Jilin	2392486.26	29.42	1.65	608862.29	50.49	1.56	1783623.97	23.51	1.68
Heilongjiang	3432219.94	23.30	2.36	718572.37	26.68	1.84	2713647.57	22.43	2.55
Anhui	4382486.75	22.69	3.02	1196167.49	36.57	3.07	3186319.26	18.18	3.00
Jiangxi	2532587.17	35.33	1.74	692438.35	56.91	1.78	1840148.82	28.68	1.73
Henan	7932837.71	40.31	5.46	1347209.82	37.84	3.46	6585627.89	40.82	6.19
Hebei	5003281.77	34.34	3.44	982092.30	42.39	2.52	4021189.47	32.52	3.78
Hunan	4385284.33	25.85	3.02	1006965.45	34.32	2.58	3378318.88	23.53	3.18
4. West Region	26061975.30	29.59	17.94	7799302.98	34.55	20.02	18262672.32	27.58	17.18
Chongqing	3210768.68	31.21	2.21	659595.53	40.17	1.69	2551173.15	29.08	2.40
Sichuan	7657702.31	32.25	5.27	1915556.72	28.80	4.92	5742145.59	33.44	5.40
Guizhou	1226271.16	28.77	0.84	469215.92	30.15	1.20	757055.24	27.93	0.71
Yunnan	2356815.14	30.87	1.62	942197.80	38.22	2.42	1414617.34	26.40	1.33
Tibet	50585.33	26.02	0.03	41122.88	20.07	0.11	9462.45	60.61	0.01
Shaanxi	3338080.29	28.59	2.30	854237.23	41.13	2.19	2483843.06	24.77	2.34
Gansu	1463353.77	27.93	1.01	388223.64	43.50	1.00	1075130.13	23.11	1.01
Qinghai	256967.98	41.13	0.18	103795.06	30.36	0.27	153172.92	49.50	0.14
Ningxia	527466.25	34.29	0.36	175019.64	47.80	0.45	352446.61	28.46	0.33
Xinjiang	1909238.66	21.84	1.31	630009.80	21.57	1.62	1279228.86	21.98	1.20
Inner Mongolia	2155372.16	25.82	1.48	962681.94	42.96	2.47	1192690.22	14.71	1.12
Guangxi	1909353.57	28.47	1.31	657646.83	32.30	1.69	1251706.74	26.55	1.18

Table 3 Insurance Penetration and Insurance Density, 2003–2010

Year	Insurance Penetration (%)	Insurance Density (RMB per Person)
2003	3.33	287.4
2004	3.39	332.2
2005	2.70	375.6
2006	2.80	431.3
2007	2.93	532.4
2008	3.25	736.7
2009	3.32	834.4
2010	3.65	1083.4

Table 4 Insurance Funds Utilization Yield 2003–2010

Year	Funds Utilization Yield（%）
2003	2.68
2004	2.87
2005	3.60
2006	5.80
2007	12.17
2008	1.91
2009	6.41
2010	4.84

Table 5 List of Insurance Asset Management Companies in 2010

Rank	Name
1	PICC Asset Management Company Limited
2	China Life Asset Management Company Limited
3	China Reinsurance (Group) Corporation
4	PingAn Asset Management Co., Ltd.
5	Huatai Asset Management Company Ltd.
6	Taikang Asset Management Co., Ltd.
7	New China Asset Management Co., Ltd.
8	Pacific Asset Management Co., Ltd.
9	Taiping Asset Management Co., Ltd.

Table 6 Top Ten Insurance Brokers by Brokerage in 2010

Rank	Name	Business Income (RMB 10000)	Market Share（%）
1	Chang'an Insurance Brokers Co., Ltd.	46666.6	10.6
2	Beijing Union Insurance Broker Co., Ltd.	34701.4	7.9
3	Jiang Tai Insurance Broker Co., Ltd.	22369.5	5.1
4	Aon-COFCO Insurance Brokers Co., Ltd.	20052.0	4.6
5	Willis Insurance Brokers Co., Ltd	18530.2	4.2
6	Marsh (Beijing) Insurance Brokers Co., Ltd.	18306.9	4.2
7	Jingsheng Insurance Brokers Co., Ltd.	14939.6	3.4
8	Huatai Insurance Agency & Consultant Service Ltd.	10663.8	2.4
9	Zhongsheng International Insurance Brokers Co., Ltd.	9211.9	2.1
10	China Insurance Brokers Co., Ltd.	9063.5	2.1

Table 7 Top Ten Insurance Agents by Business Income in 2010

Rank	Name	Business Income (RMB 10000)	Market Share (%)
1	Huakang Insurance Agency Co., Ltd.	45176.6	7.2
2	D.Tong Insurance Sales & Service Ltd.	20496.5	3.3
3	Hebei Shengan Insurance Agency Co., Ltd.	12473.9	2.0
4	Guangdong Fanhua Nanfeng Insurance Agency Co., Ltd.	10659.5	1.7
5	Sichuan CNINSURE Agency Co., Ltd.	9567.6	1.5
6	Dongguan Nanfeng Jiayu Insurance Agency Co., Ltd.	7891.9	1.3
7	Sichuan Taiyuan Insurance Agency Co., Ltd.	7534.7	1.2
8	Hebei Fanlian Insurance Agency Co., Ltd.	7434.7	1.2
9	Guangzhou Fanhua Yi'an Insurance Agency Co., Ltd.	7219.0	1.1
10	Guangzhou Huixin Insurance Agency Co., Ltd.	5032.1	0.8

Table 8 Top Ten Insurance Surveyors and Loss Adjusters Companies by Business Income in 2010

Rank	Name	Business Income (RMB 10000)	Market Share (%)
1	Shenzhen Mintai'an Insurance Surveyors & Loss Adjusters Co., Ltd.	21244.3	18.2
2	CNINSURE INC.	13927.8	12.0
3	Shenzhen Liansheng Insurance Surveyors & Loss Adjusters Co., Ltd.	4454.3	3.8
4	Shanghai Highlevels Surveying Co., Ltd.	4168.5	3.6
5	Shenzhen Zhixinda Insurance Surveyors & Loss Adjusters Co., Ltd.	4003.5	3.4
6	Cunningham Lidsey (China) Co., Ltd.	3739.0	3.2
7	Shanghai Teamhead Surveyors Co., Ltd.	3458.4	3.0
8	Beijing Huatai Insurance Surveyors & Loss Adjusters Co., Ltd.	2554.1	2.2
9	Guangdong Henglianghang Insurance Surveyors & Loss Adjusters Co., Ltd.	2352.3	2.0
10	Guangzhou Hizom Insurance Surveyors & Loss Adjusters Co., Ltd.	2159.1	1.9

>>Appendix 5

Major Economic and Financial Websites in China

The People's Bank of China: http://www.pbc.gov.cn
China Banking Regulatory Commission: http://www.cbrc.gov.cn
China Securities Regulatory Commission: http://www.csrc.gov.cn
China Insurance Regulatory Commission: http://www.circ.gov.cn
National Development and Reform Commission: http://www.ndrc.gov.cn
Ministry of Finance of People's Republic of China: http://www.mof.gov.cn
Ministry of Human Resources and Social Security of the People's Republic of China: http://www.mohrss.gov.cn
National Bureau of Statistics of China: http://www.stats.gov.cn

图书在版编目（CIP）数据

2010—2011中国保险市场年报（2010—2011 Zhongguo Baoxian Shichang Nianbao）/中国保险监督管理委员会编．—北京：中国金融出版社，2011.6

ISBN 978-7-5049-5972-0

Ⅰ. ①2… Ⅱ. ①中… Ⅲ. ①保险市场—研究报告—中国—2010—2011
Ⅳ. ①F842.6

中国版本图书馆CIP数据核字(2011)第111472号

出版
发行 中国金融出版社

社址 北京市丰台区益泽路2号

市场开发部 (010)63266347，63805472，63439533（传真）

网上书店 http://www.chinafph.com (010)63286832，63365686（传真）

读者服务部 (010)66070833，62568380

邮编 100071

经销 新华书店

印刷 北京松源印刷有限公司

尺寸 210毫米×296毫米

印张 5.25

字数 170千

版次 2011年6月第1版

印次 2011年6月第1次印刷

定价 120.00元

ISBN 978-7-5049-5972-0/F.5532